MICAH, ZEPHANIAH, NAHUM, HABAKKUK, JOEL & OBADIAH

God's Comfort for His People

John MacArthur

HarperChristian
Resources

MacArthur Bible Studies
Micah, Zephaniah, Nahum, Habakkuk, Joel and Obadiah: God's Comfort for His People
© 2024 by John MacArthur

Published in Grand Rapids, Michigan, by HarperChristian Resources. HarperChristian Resources
is a registered trademark of HarperCollins Christian Publishing, Inc.

Requests for information should be sent to customercare@harpercollins.com.

ISBN 978-0-310-12388-0 (softcover)
ISBN 978-0-310-12389-7 (ebook)

HarperChristian Resources titles may be purchased in bulk for church, business, fundraising,
or ministry use. For information, please e-mail ResourceSpecialist@ChurchSource.com.

Some material from the Introduction, "Keys to the Text," and "Exploring the Meaning" sections are taken
from The MacArthur Bible Commentary, John MacArthur. Copyright © 2005 Thomas Nelson Publishers.

First Printing July 2024 / Printed in the United States of America

24 25 26 27 28 LBC 5 4 3 2 1

CONTENTS

INTRODUCTION

The books of Micah, Zephaniah, Nahum, Habakkuk, Joel, and Obadiah are among the "minor prophets" in the Bible. The term was introduced in connection with the relative length of these prophetic works. The "major prophets" of the Bible—including Isaiah, Jeremiah, Ezekiel, and Daniel—produced longer tomes that covered a large number of verses on a wide range of topics. The minor prophets, by comparison, wrote much shorter books—some even as short as a single chapter. Importantly, the size of their prophecies do not lessen the importance of their message; each prophet wrote under the inspiration of the Holy Spirit.

We know relatively little about most of the minor prophets, including those whose books are covered in this study. Some were likely farmers who received God's call to share His message with the power brokers of Israel and Judah. Some may have been priests or Levites. Zephaniah was a descendant of King Hezekiah of Judah, but little else is known about him. All we know about Nahum is that he was "an Elkoshite," likely referring to his hometown.

In short, the minor prophets are relatively obscure figures, given the scope of history. Yet, in many ways, that was the point of their ministry. They were not important because of their connections or their wealth or their volumes of prose. They became important because they faithfully spoke the words of God to those who needed to hear them.

THE BOOK OF MICAH

The name of the book is derived from the prophet who, having received the Word of the Lord, was commissioned to proclaim it. Micah, whose name is shared by others in the Old Testament (see Judges 17:1; 2 Chronicles 13:2;

Jeremiah 36:11), is a shortened form of Micaiah (or Michaiah) and means "Who is like the LORD?" The prophet employs a play on his own name in 7:18, saying, "Who is a God like You?"

AUTHOR AND DATE

Little is known about Micah. His parentage is not given, but his name suggests a godly heritage. He traces his roots to the town of Moresheth (see 1:1, 14), which was located in the foothills of Judah, approximately twenty-five miles southwest of Jerusalem, on the border of Judah and Philistia near Gath. Much like the prophet Amos, he was from a productive agricultural area; a country resident removed from the national politics and religion yet chosen by God (see 3:8) to deliver a message of judgment to the princes and people of Jerusalem.

Micah places his prophecy during the reigns of Jotham (750–731 BC), Ahaz (731–715 BC), and Hezekiah (715–686 BC), each of whom were kings of Judah. Micah's indictments of social injustices and religious corruption renew the theme of Amos (who ministered in the mid-eighth century BC) and of his contemporaries: Hosea in the north (c. 755–710 BC) and Isaiah in the south (c. 739–690 BC). This fits what is known about the character of Ahaz (see 2 Kings 16:10–18) and his son Hezekiah prior to his sweeping spiritual reformations (see 2 Chronicles 29; 31:1). Micah's references to the imminent fall of Samaria (see 1:6) position him before 722 BC, c. 735–710 BC.

BACKGROUND AND SETTING

Because the northern kingdom was about to fall to Assyria during Micah's ministry in 722 BC, Micah dates his message with the mention of Judean kings only. Although Israel was an occasional recipient of his words (see 1:5–7), his primary attention was directed toward the southern kingdom in which he lived. The economic prosperity and the absence of international crises that marked the days of Jeroboam II (793–753 BC), during which the borders of Judah and Israel rivaled those of David and Solomon (see 2 Kings 14:23–27), were slipping away.

Syria and Israel invaded Judah c. 740–732 BC, taking the wicked Ahaz temporarily captive (see 2 Chronicles 28:5–16; Isaiah 7:1–2). After Assyria had overthrown Syria and Israel, the good king Hezekiah withdrew his allegiance to Assyria, causing Sennacherib to besiege Jerusalem in 701 BC (see 2 Kings 18–19; 2 Chronicles 32). The Lord then sent His angel to deliver Judah (see 2 Chronicles 32:21). Hezekiah was used by the Lord to lead Judah back to true worship.

After the prosperous reign of Uzziah, who died in 739 BC, his son Jotham continued the same policies but failed to remove the centers of idolatry. Outward prosperity was only a façade, masking rampant social corruption and religious syncretism. Woship of the Canaanite fertility god Baal was increasingly integrated with the Old Testament sacrificial system, reaching epidemic proportions under the reign of Ahaz (see 2 Chronicles 28:1–4). When Samaria fell, thousands of refugees swarmed into Judah, bringing their religious syncretism with them.

However, while Micah (like Hosea) addressed this issue, it was the disintegration of personal and social values to which he delivered his most stinging rebukes and stern warnings (see, for example, Micah 7:5–6). Assyria was the dominant power and a constant threat to Judah, so Micah's prediction that Babylon, then under Assyrian rule, would conquer Judah (see 4:10) seemed remote. Thus, as the prophet Amos was to Israel, so Micah was to Judah.

HISTORICAL AND THEOLOGICAL THEMES

Primarily, Micah proclaimed a message of judgment to a people persistently pursuing evil. Similar to other prophets (see Hosea 4:1; Amos 3:1), Micah presents his message in lawsuit/courtroom terminology (see 1:2; 6:1–2). He arranges his prophecies in three oracles or cycles, each beginning with the admonition to "hear" (1:2; 3:1; 6:1). Within each oracle, he moves from doom to hope—doom because the people had broken God's Law given at Sinai, and then hope because of God's unchanging covenant with their forefathers (7:20).

One-third of the book of Micah targets the sins of the people; another one-third looks at the punishment of God to come; and another one-third promises hope for the faithful after the judgment. Thus, the theme of the inevitability of divine judgment for sin is coupled with God's immutable commitment to His covenant promises. The combination of (1) God's absolute consistency in judging sin and (2) His unbending commitment to His covenant through the remnant of His people provides the hearers with a clear disclosure of the character of the Sovereign of the universe. Through divine intervention, He will bring about both judgment on sinners and blessing on those who repent.

INTERPRETIVE CHALLENGES

The verbal similarity between Micah 4:1–3 and Isaiah 2:2–4 raises the question of who quoted whom. Interpreters are divided, with no clear-cut evidence supporting either side. Because the two prophets lived in close proximity to each other, prophesying during the same period, this similarity is understandable. God gave the same message through two preachers. The introductory phrase, "in the latter days" (4:1), removes these verses from any post-exilic fulfillment and requires an eschatological fulfillment associated with the Second Advent of Christ and the beginning of the Millennium.

Apart from Isaiah 2:2–4, three other passages from Micah are quoted elsewhere in Scripture. Micah 3:12 is quoted in Jeremiah 26:18, thereby saving Jeremiah's life from King Jehoiakim's death sentence. Micah 5:2 is quoted by the chief priests and scribes (see Matthew 2:6) in response to Herod's query about the birthplace of the Messiah. Micah 7:6 is employed by Jesus in Matthew 10:35–36 when commissioning His disciples.

THE BOOK OF ZEPHANIAH

As with each of the twelve minor prophets, the prophecy bears the name of its author, which is generally thought to mean "the LORD hides" (see 2:3).

AUTHOR AND DATE

Little is known about the prophet Zephaniah. Three other Old Testament individuals share his name (see 2 Kings 25:18; 1 Chronicles 6:36; Jeremiah 21:1). He traces his genealogy back four generations to King Hezekiah (c. 715–686 BC), standing alone among the prophets descended from royal blood (see Zephaniah 1:1). Royal genealogy would have given him the ear of Judah's King Josiah, during whose reign he preached.

The prophet himself dates his message during the reign of Josiah (640–609 BC). The moral and spiritual conditions detailed in the book (see 1:4–6; 3:1–7) seem to place the prophecy prior to Josiah's reforms, when Judah was still languishing in idolatry and wickedness. It was in 628 BC that Josiah tore down all the altars to Baal, burned the bones of false prophets, and broke the carved idols (see 2 Chronicles 34:3–7); and in 622 BC, the Book of the Law was found (see 2 Chronicles 34:8–35:19). Consequently, Zephaniah most likely prophesied from 635–625 BC and was a contemporary of Jeremiah.

BACKGROUND AND SETTING

Politically, the imminent transfer of Assyrian world power to the Babylonians weakened Nineveh's hold on Judah, bringing an element of independence to Judah for the first time in fifty years. King Josiah's desire to retain this newfound

freedom from taxation and subservience undoubtedly led him to later inter-
fere with Egypt's attempt to interdict the fleeing king of Nineveh in 609 BC (see
2 Chronicles 35:20–27). Spiritually, the reigns of Hezekiah's son Manasseh (c.
695–642 BC), extending over four decades, and his grandson Amon (c. 642–
640 BC), lasting only two years, were marked by wickedness and apostasy (see
2 Kings 21; 2 Chronicles 33).

The early years of Josiah's reign were also characterized by the evil from his
father (see 2 Kings 23:4). However, in 622 BC, while repairing the house of the
Lord, Hilkiah the high priest found the Book of the Law (see 2 Kings 22:8).
Upon reading it, Josiah initiated extensive reforms (see 2 Kings 23). It was
during the early years of Josiah's reign, prior to the great revival, that Zephaniah,
this eleventh-hour prophet, prophesied and no doubt had an influence on the
sweeping reforms that Josiah brought to the nation. But the evil kings before
Josiah—Amon and Manasseh, who reigned some fifty-five years (see 2 Kings
21)—had such an adverse effect on Judah that it never recovered. Josiah's reforms were too late and didn't outlast his life.

HISTORICAL AND THEOLOGICAL THEMES

Zephaniah's message about the Day of the Lord warned Judah that its final days
were near, through divine judgment at the hands of Nebuchadnezzar, c. 605–
586 BC (see 1:4–13). Yet the prophet's message also looked beyond to the far
fulfillment in the judgments of Daniel's seventieth week (see 1:18; 3:8). The
expression "Day of the Lord" is described as a day that is near (see 1:7) and
as a day of wrath, trouble, distress, devastation, desolation, darkness, gloominess, clouds, thick darkness, trumpet, and alarm (see 1:15–16, 18). However,
even within these oracles of divine wrath, the prophet exhorts the people to seek
the Lord, offering a shelter in the midst of judgment (see 2:3), and proclaiming
the promise of eventual salvation for His believing remnant (see 2:7; 3:9–20).

INTERPRETIVE CHALLENGES

The prophet Zephaniah presents an unambiguous denunciation of sin and
warning of imminent judgment on the nation of Judah. Some have interpreted
the phrase "I will restore to the peoples a pure language" (3:9) as the restoration of a universal language, similar to the days prior to confusion of lan-
guages at the Tower of Babel (see Genesis 11:1–9). They point out that the
word "language" is also used in Genesis 11:7.

It is better, however, to understand the passage as pointing to a purification of heart and life. This is confirmed by the context (see Zephaniah 3:13) and corroborated by the fact that the word "language" is most commonly translated "lip." When combined with "pure," the reference to speech speaks of inward cleansing from sin (see Isaiah 6:5) manifested in speech (see Matthew 12:34), including the removal of the names of false gods from their lips (see Hosea 2:17). It does not imply a one-world language.

THE BOOK OF NAHUM

The book's title is taken from the prophet's oracle against Nineveh, the capital of Assyria. Nahum means "comfort" or "consolation" and is a short form of Nehemiah ("comfort of Yahweh"). Nahum is not quoted in the New Testament, though there may be an allusion to Nahum 1:15 in Romans 10:15 (see also Isaiah 52:7).

AUTHOR AND DATE

The significance of the writing prophets was not their personal lives; it was their message. Thus, background information about the prophets from within their prophecies are rare. Occasionally, one of the historical books will shed some additional light. In the case of Nahum, nothing is provided except that he was an Elkoshite (see Nahum 1:1), referring either to his birthplace or his place of ministry. Attempts to identify the location of Elkosh have been unsuccessful. Suggestions include Al Qosh, situated in northern Iraq (thus Nahum would have been a descendant of the exiles taken to Assyria in 722 BC), Capernaum ("town of Nahum"), or a location in southern Judah (see 1:15). His birthplace or locale is not significant to the interpretation of the book.

There is no mention of any kings in the introduction to the book of Nahum, so the date of his prophecy must be implied by historical data. The message of judgment against Nineveh portrays a nation of strength, intimating a time not only prior to her fall in 612 BC but also probably before the death of Ashurbanipal in 626 BC, after which Assyria's power declined rapidly. Nahum's mention of the fall of No Amon, also called Thebes (see 3:8–10), in 663 BC (at the hands of Ashurbanipal) appears to be fresh in their minds. There is also no mention of the rekindling that occurred ten years later, suggesting a mid-seventh century BC date during the reign of Manasseh (c. 695–642 BC; see 2 Kings 21:1–18).

BACKGROUND AND SETTING

A century after Nineveh repented at the preaching of Jonah, she returned to idolatry, violence, and arrogance (see Nahum 3:1–4). Assyria was at the height of power, having recovered from Sennacherib's defeat (701 BC) at Jerusalem (see Isaiah 37:36–38). Her borders extended all the way into Egypt. Esarhaddon had recently transplanted conquered peoples into Samaria and Galilee in 670 BC (see 2 Kings 17:24; Ezra 4:2), leaving Syria and Palestine very weak. But God brought Nineveh down under the rising power of Babylon's king Nabopolassar and his son Nebuchadnezzar (c. 612 BC). Assyria's demise turned out just as God had prophesied.

HISTORICAL AND THEOLOGICAL THEMES

Nahum forms a sequel to the book of Jonah, who prophesied more than a century earlier. Jonah recounts the remission of God's promised judgment toward Nineveh, while Nahum depicts the later execution of God's judgment. Nineveh was proud of her reputed invulnerable city, her walls reaching one hundred feet high and with a moat 150 feet wide and sixty feet deep. However, Nahum established the fact that the sovereign God (see 1:2–5) would bring vengeance upon those who violated His law (see 1:8, 14; 3:5–7). The same God had a retributive judgment against evil that is also redemptive, bestowing His loving kindnesses upon the faithful (see 1:7, 12–13, 15; 2:2).

The prophecy brought comfort to the people of Judah and to all who feared the cruel Assyrians. Nahum said Nineveh would end "with an overflowing flood" (1:8), and this happened when the Tigris River overflowed to destroy enough of the walls to let the Babylonians through them. Nahum also predicted that the city would be hidden (see 3:11). After its destruction in 612 BC, the site was not rediscovered until AD 1842.

INTERPRETIVE CHALLENGES

Apart from the uncertain identity of Elkosh, the prophecy presents no real interpretive difficulties. The book is a straightforward prophetic announcement of judgment against Assyria and her capital, Nineveh, for cruel atrocities and idolatrous practices.

THE BOOK OF HABAKKUK

This prophetic book takes its name from its author and possibly means "one who embraces" (see 1:1; 3:1). By the end of the prophecy, this name becomes appropriate, as the prophet clings to God regardless of his confusion about God's plans for His people.

AUTHOR AND DATE

As with many of the minor prophets, nothing is known about the prophet except what can be inferred from the book. In the case of Habakkuk, internal information is virtually nonexistent, making conclusions about his identity and life conjectural at best. His simple introduction as "the prophet Habakkuk" may imply that he needed no introduction, since he was a well-known prophet of his day. It is certain that he was a contemporary of Jeremiah, Ezekiel, Daniel, and Zephaniah.

Habakkuk's mention of the Chaldeans—better known to history as the Babylonians (see 1:6)—suggests a late seventh century BC date, shortly before Nebuchadnezzar began his military march through Nineveh (612 BC), Haran (609 BC), and Carchemish (605 BC), on his way to Jerusalem (605 BC). Habakkuk's bitter lament (see 1:2–4) may reflect a time period shortly after the death of Josiah (609 BC), days in which the godly king's reforms (see 2 Kings 23) were quickly overturned by his successor, Jehoiakim (see Jeremiah 22:13–19).

BACKGROUND AND SETTING

Habakkuk prophesied during the final days of the Assyrian Empire and the beginning of Babylon's world rulership under Nabopolassar and his son Nebuchadnezzar. When Nabopolassar ascended to power in 626 BC, he immediately began to expand his influence to the north and west. Under the leadership of his son, the Babylonian army overthrew Nineveh in 612 BC, forcing the Assyrian nobility to take refuge, first in Haran and then Carchemish. Nebuchadnezzar pursued them, overrunning Haran in 609 BC and Carchemish in 605 BC.

The Egyptian king Necho, traveling through Judah in 609 BC to assist the fleeing Assyrian king, was opposed by King Josiah at Megiddo (2 Chronicles 35:20–24). Josiah was killed in the ensuing battle, leaving his throne to a succession of three sons and a grandson. Earlier, as a result of discovering the Book of the Law in the temple (622 BC), Josiah had instituted significant spiritual reforms in Judah (see 2 Kings 22–23), abolishing many of the idolatrous practices of his father, Amon (see 2 Kings 21:20–22), and grandfather, Manasseh (see 2 Kings 21:11–13). Upon his death, however, the nation quickly reverted to her evil ways (see Jeremiah 22:13–19), causing Habakkuk to question God's silence and apparent lack of punitive action (see 1:2–4) to purge His covenant people.

HISTORICAL AND THEOLOGICAL THEMES

The opening verses reveal a historical situation similar to the days of Amos and Micah. Justice had essentially disappeared from the land. Violence and wickedness were pervasive, existing unchecked. In the midst of these dark days, the prophet Habakkuk cried out for divine intervention (see 1:2–4). God's response—that He was sending the Babylonians to judge Judah (see 1:5–11)—creates an even greater theological dilemma for Habakkuk: Why didn't God purge His people and restore their righteousness? How could God use the Babylonians to judge a people more righteous than they (see 1:12–2:1)?

God's answer that He would also judge the Babylonians (see 2:2–20) did not fully satisfy the prophet's theological quandary; in fact, it only intensified it. In Habakkuk's mind, the issue crying for resolution was no longer God's righteous response toward evil (or lack thereof) but the vindication of God's character and covenant with His people (see 1:13). Like Job, the prophet argued with God and, through that experience, achieved a deeper understanding of God's sovereign character and a firmer faith in Him (see Job 42:5–6; Isaiah 55:8–9). Ultimately, Habakkuk realized that God was not to be worshiped merely because of the temporal blessings He bestowed but for His own sake (see 3:17–19).

INTERPRETIVE CHALLENGES

The queries of the prophet represent some of the most fundamental questions in all of life, with the answers providing crucial foundation stones on which to build a proper understanding of God's character and His sovereign ways in history. The core of Habakkuk's message lies in the call to trust God—"the just shall live by his faith" (2:4).

The New Testament references ascribe unusual importance theologically to Habakkuk. The writer of Hebrews quotes Habakkuk 2:4 to amplify the believer's need to remain strong and faithful in the midst of affliction and trials (see Hebrews 10:38). The apostle Paul, on the other hand, uses the verse twice (see Romans 1:17; Galatians 3:11) to accentuate the doctrine of justification by faith. There need not be any interpretive conflict, however, for the emphasis in both Habakkuk and the New Testament references goes beyond the act of faith to include the continuity of faith. Faith is not a one-time act, but a way of life. The true believer, declared righteous by God, will habitually persevere in faith throughout all his life (see Colossians 1:22–23; Hebrews 3:12–14). He will trust the sovereign God who only does what is right.

THE BOOK OF JOEL

The Greek Septuagint (LXX) and Latin Vulgate versions follow the Hebrew Masoretic Text, titling this book after Joel the prophet, who received this message from God (see 1:1). The name means "the Lord is God" and refers to at least a dozen other men in the Old Testament (see, for example, 1 Samuel 8:2; 1 Chronicles 4:35; 5:4, 12; 6:36; 7:3; 11:38; 15:7; 27:20; 2 Chronicles 29:12; Ezra 10:43; Nehemiah 11:9). Joel is referred to only once in the New Testament (see Acts 2:16–21).

AUTHOR AND DATE

The author identified himself only as "Joel the son of Pethuel" (1:1). The prophecy provides little else about him. Even the name of his father is not mentioned elsewhere in the Old Testament. Although Joel displayed a profound zeal for the temple sacrifices (see 1:9; 2:13–16), his familiarity with pastoral and agricultural life and his separation from the priests (see 1:13–14; 2:17) suggest he was not a Levite. Extrabiblical tradition records that he was from the tribe of Reuben, from the town of Bethom or Bethharam, located northeast of the Dead Sea on the border of Reuben and Gad. The context of the prophecy, however, hints that he was a Judean from the Jerusalem vicinity, since the tone of a stranger is absent.

Dating the book relies solely on canonical position, historical allusions, and linguistic elements. Because of (1) the lack of any explicit mention of later world powers (Assyria, Babylon, or Persia); (2) the fact that Joel's style is like that of Hosea and Amos, rather than of the post-exilic prophets; and (3) the verbal parallels with other early prophets (Joel 3:16/Amos 1:2; Joel 3:18/Amos 9:13), a late-ninth-century-BC date, during the reign of Joash (c. 835–796 BC), seems most convincing. Nevertheless, while the date of the book cannot be known with certainty, the impact on its interpretation is minimal. The message of Joel is timeless, forming doctrine that could be repeated and applied in any age.

BACKGROUND AND SETTING

Tyre, Sidon, and Philistia had made frequent military incursions into Israel (see Joel 3:2ff.). An extended drought and massive invasion of locusts had stripped every green thing from the land and brought severe economic devastation (see 1:7–20), leaving the southern kingdom weak. This physical disaster gives Joel the illustration for God's judgment. As the locusts were a judgment on sin, God's future judgments during the Day of the Lord will far exceed them. In that day, God will judge His enemies and bless the faithful. No mention is made of specific sins, nor is Judah rebuked for idolatry. Yet, possibly due to a calloused indifference, the prophet calls them to repentance, admonishing them to "rend your heart, and not your garments" (2:13).

HISTORICAL AND THEOLOGICAL THEMES

The theme of Joel is the Day of the Lord. The phrase is employed nineteen times by eight different Old Testament authors (Isaiah 2:12; 13:6, 9; Ezekiel 13:5; 30:3; Joel 1:15; 2:1, 11, 31; 3:14; Amos 5:18 [2 times], 20; Obadiah 1:15; Zephaniah 1:7, 14 [2 times]; Zechariah 14:1; Malachi 4:5), and appears four times in the New Testament (Acts 2:20; 1 Thessalonians 5:2; 2 Thessalonians 2:2; 2 Peter 3:10), but it permeates all parts of Joel's message (see 1:15; 2:1; 2:11; 2:31; 3:14), making it the most sustained treatment of the topic in the entire Old Testament. The phrase does not have reference to a chronological time period but to a general period of wrath and judgment uniquely belonging to the Lord. It is exclusively the day that unveils His character—mighty, powerful, and holy, thus terrifying His enemies.

The Day of the Lord does not always refer to an eschatological event; on occasion it has a near historical fulfillment, as seen in Ezekiel 13:5, where it speaks of the Babylonian conquest and destruction of Jerusalem. As is common in prophecy, the near fulfillment is a historic event that gives understanding to the more distant, eschatological fulfillment.

The Day of the Lord is frequently associated with seismic disturbances (see, for example, Joel 2:1–11; 2:30; 3:16), violent weather (see Ezekiel 13:5ff.), clouds and thick darkness (see, for example, Joel 2:2; Zephaniah 1:7ff.), cosmic upheaval (see Joel 2:3, 30), and as a "great and very terrible" (2:11) day that would "come as destruction from the Almighty" (1:15). The latter portion of Joel (2:18–3:21) depicts time immediately prior to and subsequent to the Day of the Lord in terms of promise and hope. There will be a pouring out of the Spirit on all flesh, accompanied by prophetic utterances, dreams, and visions (see 2:28–29).

As a result of the Day of the Lord, there will be physical blessings, fruitfulness, and prosperity (see 2:21ff.; 3:16–21). It is a day when judgment is poured out on sinners that subsequently leads to blessings on the penitent and reaffirmation of God's covenant with His people.

INTERPRETIVE CHALLENGES

First, what is the relationship of chapter 2 to chapter 1? It is preferable to view chapter 1 as describing an actual, historical invasion of locusts that devastated the land. In chapter 2, a heightened level of description engages the interpreter. Here the prophet is projecting something beyond the locust plague of chapter 1, elevating the level of description with increased intensity that is focused on the plague and the immediate necessity for true repentance. The prophet's choice of similes, such as "like the appearance of horses" (2:4) and "like mighty men" (2:7), suggests that he is still using the actual locusts to illustrate an invasion that can only be the massive onslaught of the final Day of the Lord.

A second issue facing the interpreter is Peter's quotation from Joel 2:28–32 in Acts 2:16–21. Some have viewed the miraculous phenomena of Acts 2 and the destruction of Jerusalem in AD 70 as the final fulfillment of the Joel passage, while others have reserved its ultimate fulfillment to the final Day of the Lord only— but clearly, Joel is primarily referring to the final, terrible Day of the Lord. The pouring out of the Holy Spirit at Pentecost was not the entire fulfillment but rather a preview and sample of the Spirit's power and work to be released fully and finally in the Messiah's kingdom after the Day of the Lord.

Third, the time perspective (historical or eschatological) of various portions in Joel is sometimes questioned. The discussion that follows will help to clarify. After Joel 1:1, the contents of the book are arranged under three basic categories. In the first section (1:2–20), the prophet describes the contemporary Day of the Lord. The land is suffering massive devastation caused by a locust plague and drought. The details of the calamity (verses 2–12) are followed by a summons to communal penitence and reformation (verses 13–20).

The second section (2:1–17) provides a transition from the historical plague of locusts described in chapter 1 to the eschatological Day of the Lord in 2:18– 3:21. Employing the contemporary infestation of locusts as a backdrop, the prophet, with a raised level of intensity, paints a vivid and forceful picture of the impending visitation of the Lord (2:1–11) and, with powerful and explicit termi-nology, tenaciously renews the appeal for repentance (2:12–17).

In the third section (2:18–3:21), the Lord speaks directly of an eschatological hope, assuring His people of His presence among them (see 2:27; 3:17, 21). This portion of Joel assumes that the repentance solicited (see 2:12–17) had occurred and describes the Lord's zealous response (see 2:18–19a) to their prayer. Joel 2:18–20 forms the transition in the message from lamentation and woe to divine assurances of God's presence and the reversal of the calamities, with 2:19b–20 in-troducing the essence and nature of that reversal. The Lord then gives three promises to assure the penitents of His presence: (1) material restoration through the divine healing of their land (see 2:21–27), (2) spiritual restoration through the divine outpouring of His Spirit (see 2:28–32), and (3) national restoration through the divine judgment on the unrighteous (see 3:1–21).

THE BOOK OF OBADIAH

The book of Obadiah is named after the prophet who received the vision (see 1:1). Obadiah means "servant of the Lord" and occurs twenty times in the Old Testament, referring to many other Old Testament individuals (see, for example, 1 Kings 18:3; 1 Chronicles 3:21; 8:38; 9:16; 12:9; 27:19; 2 Chronicles 17:7; 34:12; Ezra 8:9; Nehemiah 10:5; 12:25). Obadiah is the shortest book in the Old Testament and is not quoted in the New Testament.

AUTHOR AND DATE

Nothing is known for certain about the author. Other Old Testament references to at least eleven men with this name do not appear to be referring to this prophet. His frequent mentions of Jerusalem, Judah, and Zion suggest that he belonged to the southern kingdom (see 1:10–12, 17, 21). Obadiah was probably a contemporary of Elijah and Elisha.

The date of writing is equally difficult to determine, though it is associated with the Edomite assault on Jerusalem described in 1:10–14. Obadiah apparently wrote shortly after the attack. There were four significant invasions of Jerusalem recorded in Old Testament history: (1) by Shishak, king of Egypt, c. 925 BC during the reign of Rehoboam (see 1 Kings 14:25–26; 2 Chronicles 12); (2) by the Philistines and Arabians between 848–841 BC, during the reign of Jehoram of Judah (see 2 Chronicles 21:8–20); (3) by Jehoash, king of Israel, c. 790 BC (see 2 Kings 14; 2 Chronicles 25); and (4) by Nebuchadnezzar, king of Babylon, in the fall of Jerusalem in 586 BC.

Of these four, only the second and the fourth fit the historical data. Number two is preferable, since Obadiah's description does not indicate the absolute, total destruction of the city, which took place under Nebuchadnezzar's attack. Also, although the Edomites were involved in Nebuchadnezzar's destruction of Jerusalem (see Psalm 137; Lamentations 4:21), it is significant that Obadiah does not mention the Babylonians by name (as with all the other prophets who wrote about Jerusalem's fall), nor is there any reference to the destruction of the temple or the deportation of the people. In fact, the captives appear to have been taken to the southwest, not east to Babylon (see Obadiah 1:20).

BACKGROUND AND SETTING

The Edomites trace their origin to Esau, the firstborn (twin) son of Isaac and Rebekah (see Genesis 25:24–26), who struggled with Jacob even while in the womb (see 25:22). Esau's name means "hairy," because "he was like a hairy garment all over" (25:25). He is also called Edom, meaning "red," owing to the sale of his birthright in exchange for some "red stew" (see 25:30). Esau showed a disregard for the covenant promises by marrying two Canaanite women (see 26:34), and later the daughter of Ishmael (see 28:9). He loved the out-of-doors and, after having his father's blessing stolen from him by Jacob, was destined to remain a man of the open spaces (see 25:27; 27:38–40).

Esau settled in a region of mostly rugged mountains south of the Dead Sea (see Genesis 33:16; 36:8–9; Deuteronomy 2:4–5) called Edom (Greek "Idumea"), the forty-mile-wide area that stretches approximately one hundred miles south to the Gulf of Aqabah. The famed King's Highway, an essential caravan route linking North Africa with Europe and Asia, passes along the eastern plateau (see Numbers 20:17). The struggle and birth of Jacob and Esau (see Genesis 25) form the ultimate background to the prophecy of Genesis 25:23: "Two nations are in your womb." Their respective national descendants, Israel and Edom, were perpetual enemies.

When Israel came out from Egypt, Edom denied brother Jacob passage through their land, located south of the Dead Sea (see Numbers 20:14–21). Nevertheless, Israel was instructed by God to be kind to Edom (see Deuteronomy 23:7–8). Obadiah, having received a vision from God, was sent to describe Edom's crimes and to pronounce total destruction upon them because of their treatment of Israel.

The Edomites opposed Saul (c. 1043–1011 BC) and were subdued under David (c. 1011–971 BC) and Solomon (c. 971–931 BC). They fought against Jehoshaphat (c. 873–848 BC) and successfully rebelled against Jehoram (c. 853–841 BC). They were again conquered by Judah under Amaziah (c. 796–767 BC), but they regained their freedom during the reign of Ahaz (c. 735–715 BC). Edom was later controlled by Assyria and Babylon; and in the fifth century BC, the Edomites were forced by the Nabateans to leave their territory. They moved to the area of southern Palestine and became known as Idumeans.

Herod the Great, an Idumean, became king of Judea under Rome in 37 BC. In a sense, the enmity between Esau and Jacob was continued in Herod's attempt to murder Jesus as a baby (see Matthew 2:16). The Idumeans participated in the rebellion of Jerusalem against Rome and were defeated along with the Jews by Titus in AD 70. Ironically, the Edomites applauded the destruction of Jerusalem in 586 BC (see Psalm 137:7), but died trying to defend it in AD 70. After that time, they were never heard of again. As Obadiah predicted, they would be "cut off forever" (verse 10) and "no survivor shall remain of the house of Esau" (verse 18).

HISTORICAL AND THEOLOGICAL THEMES

Obadiah is a case study of the curses/blessings in Genesis 12:1–3, with two interrelated themes. The first theme is the judgment of Edom by God for cursing Israel. This was apparently told to Judah, thereby providing reassurance that the Lord would bring judgment upon Edom for her pride and for her participation in Judah's downfall. The second theme is Judah's restoration. This would even include the territory of the Edomites (see Obadiah 1:19–21; Isaiah 11:14). Obadiah's blessing for Judah includes the near fulfillment of Edom's demise (see verses 1–14) and the far fulfillment of the nations' judgment and Israel's final possession of Edom (see verses 15–21).

INTERPRETIVE CHALLENGES

The striking similarities (there are at least seven) between Obadiah 1:1–9 and Jeremiah 49:7–22 brings up the question of who borrowed from whom. Assuming that there was not a third common source (which is a remote possibility), it appears that Jeremiah borrowed, where appropriate, from Obadiah, because the shared verses form one unit in Obadiah, while in Jeremiah they are scattered among other verses. This would corroborate the "setting" conclusion that Obadiah preceded Jeremiah by about 250 years, thus making it impossible for Obadiah to have borrowed from Jeremiah.

1

THE COURTROOM
Micah 1:1–2:13

DRAWING NEAR

What are ways you prefer to have bad news delivered to you? In other words, what methods of receiving bad news makes it the easiest for you to swallow?

_____

_____

_____

_____

_____

_____

_____

_____

_____

_____

_____

_____

THE CONTEXT

If it is correct that Micah ministered as a prophet from 735–710 BC, it would mean that he was alive when the Assyrian army conquered the northern kingdom of Israel in 722 BC and ransacked its capital city of Samaria. Micah may have also experienced Assyria's siege against Jerusalem in 701 BC. This attempt to destroy the holy city ultimately failed thanks to God's intervention, yet Micah would have experienced firsthand the terrors of siege warfare.

For these reasons and more, Micah understood the stakes involved with Judah's idolatrous pursuits and continued rebellion against God. Even as the residents of Jerusalem stubbornly refused to believe that God would allow true judgment against Zion, Micah knew the truth. His mission was to communicate that truth to those who did not want to hear it.

Importantly, Micah did not offer his opinions to the residents of Judah and Jerusalem. Instead, operating as a true prophet, he spoke the words of God. He shared visions and prophecies given to him by the Holy Spirit. In carrying out this important work, his singular goal was to call God's people to repentance so that they might be saved from destruction.

KEYS TO THE TEXT

Read Micah 1:1–2:13, noting the key words and phrases indicated below.

> SAMARIA AND JUDAH PUNISHED: *Micah summons all the nations of the world into court to hear charges against Samaria and Judah. Their destruction is to be a warning example to them, prefiguring God's judgment on all who sin against Him.*

1:1. MORESHETH: A town located southwest of Jerusalem, near the Philistine city of Gath (see verse 14).

2. HIS HOLY TEMPLE: The context points to God's heavenly throne (see Psalm 11:4; Isaiah 6:1, 4).

3–4. HIGH PLACES . . . MOUNTAINS: These could refer to key military positions, so crucial to Israel's defense, or to the pagan places of worship in the land (see verse 5). When fortifications disappeared like melted wax, the people would be gripped by the terrifying reality that they were to answer to the Judge of all the earth (see Genesis 18:25; Amos 4:12–13).

3. THE LORD IS COMING . . . HE WILL COME DOWN: A warning of impending divine judgment by the One who sits in the ultimate high place. As an omnipotent conqueror, the sovereign Lord over all creation is assured of victory.

5. SAMARIA . . . JERUSALEM: The two capitals of Israel and Judah, here representative of their respective nations.

6–7. I WILL MAKE SAMARIA A HEAP: The Lord here speaks directly of the fall of Samaria at the hands of the Assyrians (in 722 BC).

7. PAY AS A HARLOT: Centers of idolatry were financed primarily through payments of money, food, and clothing (see Genesis 38:17–18; Ezekiel 16:10–11; Hosea 2:8–9; 3:1) to cultic prostitutes, who were strictly forbidden in Israel (see Deuteronomy 23:17–18). Precious gold and silver taken from Israel's temples was used by the Assyrian invaders for their own idol worship.

8–16. I WILL WAIL AND HOWL: The judgment was so grave that even the prophet lamented as he traced the enemy's irreversible invasion.

9. TO THE GATE OF MY PEOPLE: Assyria, under Sennacherib, came close to toppling Judah in 701 BC (see 2 Kings 18:13–27). It is best to view "my" in this verse as relating to Micah, not God, in contrast to the NKJV translation, where "my" is capitalized.

10. TELL IT NOT IN GATH: Reflective of David's dirge at Saul's death (see 2 Samuel 1:20), Micah admonished the people not to tell the Philistines, lest they would be glad and rejoice. Micah, because of the location of his upbringing, knew how they would react. Eleven towns west of Jerusalem are mentioned in verses 10–15, some with a play on words.

BETH APHRAH: Literally "house of dust."

11. SHAPHIR: Literally "beautiful."

ZAANAN: Literally "going out." The inhabitants of Zaanan, in danger and fear, would not go out to console their neighbors who had been overrun.

12. MAROTH: Literally "bitterness."

DISASTER CAME DOWN: This points to the Lord as the source of judgment (see verses 3–4).

13. LACHISH . . . SIN TO THE DAUGHTER OF ZION: Located southwest of Jerusalem, Lachish was a key military fortress whose "sin" was dependence on military might.

14. GIVE PRESENTS: As parting gifts were given to brides (see 1 Kings 9:16), so this was a symbol of the departure of Moresheth Gath into captivity.

15. GLORY OF ISRAEL . . . ADULLAM: The people of Israel (that is, her "glory"; see Hosea 9:11–13) were to flee to the caves, as David fled to the cave at Adullam (see 2 Samuel 23:13).

16. MAKE YOURSELF BALD: The priests were forbidden to make themselves bald (see Leviticus 21:5), nor were the people to imitate the heathen practice of doing so (see Deuteronomy 14:1). But here, to "make yourself bald" would

be acceptable as a sign of deep mourning (see Ezra 9:3; Job 1:20; Isaiah 22:12; Ezekiel 7:18).

> WOE TO EVILDOERS: *Just as Micah denounced sin against God in chapter 1, so he now denounces sin against man in chapter 2. Micah decries the corrupt practices of the affluent (verses 1–5) and attacks the false prophets (verses 6–11).*

2:1–2. THEY COVET FIELDS . . . ALSO HOUSES: The courtroom scene continues with the accusations now being read against the affluent: they had violated the tenth commandment (see Exodus 20:17; 22:26; 23:4–9). The poor, unable to defend themselves, were at the mercy of the wealthy.

2. HIS INHERITANCE: Property in Israel was ultimately to be permanent (see Leviticus 25:10, 13; Numbers 36:1–12; 1 Kings 21).

3–5. I AM DEVISING DISASTER: As a result of the people's sin, God would allow foreign invaders to divide their land; none of them would have the inheritance apportioned to them. As the rich took from the poor, so God would take back what He gave as judgment on the nation.

6–11. "DO NOT PRATTLE," YOU SAY TO THOSE WHO PROPHESY: Micah, a true prophet of the Lord God, was accused of childish babbling while the real babblers were the false prophets. These false prophets, who had commanded Micah to cease prophesying, would certainly not prophesy against the people's evil-doing; they would not confront them with the divine standard of holiness. Rather, their false message (verse 7) had stopped the mouths of the true prophets and had permitted the rulers to engage in social atrocities (verses 8–9), leading the people to destruction (verse 10). They didn't want true prophecies; therefore, they got what they wanted (see Isaiah 30:10). It is best to understand that Micah speaks in verse 6 and God in verses 7–11.

7. SPIRIT OF THE LORD: God responded to the evil prophets that their message affirming sin in the nation was inconsistent with the Holy Spirit and His true message to Micah (see 3:8). God's words do reward the righteous, but they also rebuke those engaging in evil deeds.

9. WOMEN OF MY PEOPLE: Most likely a reference to widows.

11. THE PRATTLER OF THIS PEOPLE: The people accepted any "prophet" who would tailor his message to their greed, wealth, and prosperity. This false prophet was the real "prattler."

12–13. ASSEMBLE ALL OF YOU: Messiah will make ready the way, removing the obstacles that might hinder His remnant's deliverance and return at the Second Advent (see Isaiah 11:15–16; 52:12).

12. REMNANT OF ISRAEL: See Micah 4:7; 5:7–8; 7:18. A small nucleus of God's people, preserved by His sovereign grace, would form a righteous remnant in the midst of the national apostasy. In Israel's history, there were always an obedient few who preserved, obeyed, and passed on God's Law. There will always be a remnant, because God will never forsake the Abrahamic covenant.

UNLEASHING THE TEXT

1) How is the coming of the Lord to judge Judah and Samaria described in Micah 1:3–4? What striking images are used in that passage?

_____

_____

_____

_____

_____

_____

2) Micah refers to the "transgression of Jacob" and the "sins of the house of Israel" (1:5). What were the people doing wrong? What was their transgression?

_____

_____

_____

_____

_____

_____

3) Micah rejected the false prophets who spoke against God's message of judgment (see 2:6–11). What motivations did they have to deceive God's people?

_____

_____

_____

_____

_____

_____

4) The final two verses of chapter 2 point to a future of hope after judgment. What specifically was God promising His people in Micah 2:12–13?

_____

_____

_____

_____

_____

_____

Exploring the Meaning

God Sees Through False Faith. We find a contrasting story in the opening chapters of Micah. On the one hand, there was prosperity in the land of Judah, a sense of stability and well-being, and a belief that things would continue to improve because the rich and powerful in charge had things under control. But Micah saw what they were not willing to see: that corruption and evil were everywhere. The rich were oppressing the poor, society had become corrupted by idol worship, and Judah's leaders were being influenced by foreign powers. Worst of all, they were treating God as a convenience—to be used when helpful and discarded when He interfered with their plans. God is patient and forgiving, but He had seen enough, and He was about to pass judgment on the people and the land. It is important for all of God's children today to likewise evaluate ourselves honestly. Are we calling out to God when it is convenient and suits our purpose but keeping Him at arm's length when His will runs contrary to our plans?

The Powerful Often Miss the Point. In Micah 2:1–5, the prophet warns the wealthy and powerful of God's coming wrath. This judgment did not come on them because wealth and power are inherently bad. Such qualities can be a blessing from God—an opportunity to demonstrate His provision for humanity (see Proverbs 11:24–25; Luke 6:38; James 2:15–16). However, the rich and powerful in Judah were doing exactly the opposite. They were using their wealth and power to build themselves up and gain more wealth and power. Even worse, they were doing so at the expense of the poor, oppressing them and making their lives an object of scorn and ridicule. As Micah wrote, "They covet fields and take them by violence, also houses, and seize them. So they oppress a man and his house, a man and his inheritance" (verse 2). Micah prophesizes that God would take everything away from these elites, leaving them with nothing. This passage reminds us that everything we have is a gift from God, and He intends us to share those gifts with others as a sign of our gratitude for receiving what we did not deserve.

God's Truth Always Prevails. The false prophets of Micah's day were advising him to "not prattle" (2:6). They wanted him to stop telling the people of God's truth so as not to upset the system of false idols, corrupt government, and unjust monetary system that had been established in the land. This was a case of bad press potentially ruining their livelihood. What these false prophets failed to recognize is that God would not sit idly by as they went about their endeavors. As Micah said to them, "Because it is defiled, it shall destroy, yes, with utter destruction" (verse 10). God will always speak His truth into our lives to redirect us back to His ways. If we refuse to listen to His truth, we will suffer the consequences. The question for us is thus whether we will listen to God when He gently tells us that the way we are heading will lead to destruction. Will we turn our backs on that way of life or continue on and risk His judgment?

REFLECTING ON THE TEXT

5) What are some similarities between the culture of Judah in Micah's day and the culture in our nation today? What are some differences?

_____

_____

_____

_____

6) What are signs or symptoms that a person is operating based on a false faith?

_____

_____

_____

7) What are some ways that wealth and power can be used to produce good in our world and generate a harvest for God's kingdom?

_____

_____

_____

_____

8) What are some of the ways that God steps in to redirect us or capture our attention when we are walking in a way that dishonors Him?

_____

_____

_____

_____

_____

PERSONAL RESPONSE

9) Where do you have opportunities to use the resources God has given you—your time, skills, authority, wealth, connections—to help advance His kingdom?

_____

_____

_____

_____

_____

10) Are there any circumstances in your life right now that could potentially represent God working to redirect you away from spiritual danger? How will you pray through those circumstances and seek the Lord's guidance in the coming days?

_____

_____

_____

_____

_____

_____

2

ISRAEL'S TRUE RULER

Micah 3:1–5:15

DRAWING NEAR

Think about some of the politicians or other leaders whom you have been excited to support over the course of your life. What were those leaders offering that caught your attention?

_____

_____

_____

_____

_____

_____

_____

_____

_____

_____

_____

_____

_____

_____

_____

_____

_____

THE CONTEXT

Like many books of the Bible, the structure of Micah's prophecy is both organized and important. The book is divided into three separate "oracles" or prophecies. Each one begins with a command for the people to listen: "Hear, all you peoples!" (1:2); "Hear now, O heads of Jacob" (3:1); "Hear now what the LORD says" (6:1). As we explored in the previous lesson, Micah's first oracle (1:2–2:13) described the imminent judgment that God had declared against Judah because of the idolatry and disobedience of its people—especially its leaders.

We will study the second oracle in this lesson, which is found in Micah 3:1–5:15. This oracle begins with another stunning repudiation of Judah's leaders, including language and imagery designed to shock the original recipients (and us today) out of complacency. The remainder of the oracle in chapters 4 and 5 is more hopeful, pointing forward to the millennial kingdom (chapter 4) and the appearance of the Messiah in Bethlehem (chapter 5).

As you read these chapters, notice the juxtaposition between Judah's leaders in Micah's day (the original hearers of the prophecy) and Judah's future leadership—including both the advent of the Messiah and His Kingship during the Millennium. In spite of the failure and idolatry of God's people in the ancient world, these passages (and many others) make it evident that Israel will be lifted up in the ages to come. "And the remnant of Jacob shall be among the Gentiles, in the midst of many peoples, like a lion among the beasts of the forest" (5:8).

KEYS TO THE TEXT

Read Micah 3:1–5:15, noting the key words and phrases indicated below.

> *THE LEADERS ARE GUILTY: Micah begins his second oracle by first addressing the "heads of Jacob" and "rulers of the house of Israel" (3:1).*

3:1–4. STRIP THE SKIN FROM MY PEOPLE . . . THEY WILL CRY TO THE LORD: These rulers of God's people should have been aware of their injustice, yet their conduct toward the poor was like the butchering of animals (see verses 2–3). Therefore, when God's judgment came and they cried out for help, the Lord would not answer.

5–7. PROPHETS WHO MAKE MY PEOPLE STRAY: False prophets (see 2:6–11) also stood guilty before the Judge because they misled the people, prophesying peace when they were fed but predicting war when they were not. Like the rulers, they were also motivated by greed. Therefore, having blinded others, they would also be struck with blindness and silence (verses 6–7).

8. POWER BY THE SPIRIT: Micah, in contrast to the false prophets, spoke by the power of God's Holy Spirit (see 2:7). Therefore, his message was authoritative and true.

9–12. HEADS . . . AND RULERS: All ruling classes were guilty: the rulers who judged for rewards (verses 9–11a); the priests who taught for hire (verse 11b); and the prophets who divined for money (verse 11c). All the while, these ruling classes were deceived into thinking the Lord would give them favor because they identified themselves with Him. Consequently, the nation would be destroyed (as fulfilled by Nebuchadnezzar in 586 BC).

12. ZION SHALL BE PLOWED LIKE A FIELD: Corrupt elders in Jeremiah's day (c. 627–570 BC) would later cite this prophecy as a reason not to kill him (see Jeremiah 26:18). They reasoned that because the people of Micah's day had not killed him, the Lord had relented on passing judgment on the land, and thus they should likewise spare Jeremiah's life to achieve the same result. But both Micah's prophecy and Jeremiah's would come true in time.

THE COMING LEADER WILL DELIVER AND RESTORE: Micah abruptly shifts from impending judgment against the people of Israel and Judah to prophecies of the future millennial kingdom ("the latter days") in which Mount Zion, the center of Messiah's coming earthly kingdom, will be raised both spiritually and physically.

4:1–3. IT SHALL COME TO PASS: Micah includes this prophecy from Isaiah 2:2–4 almost word for word, which indicates that he might have obtained it from Isaiah (see the note in the introduction). Both passages present a prophetic picture of Zion in the future messianic kingdom when all people will recognize Jerusalem as the capital of the world.

2. MANY NATIONS: People throughout the earth, not just Israel, will come as a spontaneous "flow" (verse 1) to worship the Lord in Jerusalem during the Millennium (see Zechariah 8:20–23).

3. BEAT THEIR SWORDS INTO PLOWSHARES: Because the Almighty One is ruling in Jerusalem with a rod of iron (see Psalm 2:9; Revelation 2:27; 12:5; 19:15), and because of the unprecedented fruitfulness of the land (see Amos 9:13), military hardware will no longer be needed.

4. UNDER HIS VINE . . . FIG TREE: This phrase, once employed as a description of the peaceful era of Solomon (see 1 Kings 4:25), looks forward to greater peace and prosperity during the Millennium (see Zechariah 3:10).

5. WE WILL WALK: Even if all others were walking after other gods at the present, the godly remnant of Israel would no longer pursue other gods but would walk after the true God in the millennial kingdom (see Joshua 24:15).

6–8. IN THAT DAY: This continues Micah's description of the wonderful conditions of the coming earthly kingdom of Messiah.

7. FOREVER: The Hebrew term does not always mean "without end" but signifies a long, indefinite period of time, the length of which is always determined by the context. Here it refers to the 1,000-year reign of Messiah on earth (see Revelation 20).

8. TOWER OF THE FLOCK: Repeating the motif of shepherding (see Micah 2:12–13), the phrase "tower of the flock" used here depicts the city of Jerusalem, the future dwelling place of Messiah, as watching over the people.

9–10. THERE YOU SHALL BE DELIVERED: Judah will be taken captive to Babylon (verses 9–10a), but the Lord will release them from there (verse 10b) by the edict of the Persian king Cyrus (c. 538 BC), allowing them to return to Jerusalem (see Ezra 1:2–4).

11–13. GATHER THEM LIKE SHEAVES TO THE THRESHING FLOOR: This prophecy again refers to the time of the Second Advent. The gathering of "many nations" and "many peoples" depicts the future battle of Armageddon (see Zechariah 12; 14). In that day, the Lord will empower His people (see Micah 5:7–9; Isaiah 11:14; Zechariah 14:14).

13. HORN IRON . . . HOOVES BRONZE: Using the figurative language of an animal with metal features, the Lord looked to a day when Israel would permanently defeat her enemies.

THE COMING MESSIAH: Micah continues to look forward to Christ's First Advent, an intervening time, and then beyond to the Second Advent.

5:1. STRIKE THE JUDGE OF ISRAEL: This is a reference to the capture of King Zedekiah at the hands of Babylon in 586 BC (see 2 Kings 24–25).

2. BETHLEHEM EPHRATHAH: Bethlehem was in the territory given to the tribe of Judah (see Joshua 15) and located about six miles south of Jerusalem.

It was the birthplace of David (see 1 Samuel 16:4) and later Jesus Christ (see Matthew 2:5; Luke 2:4–7). The name Bethlehem means "house of bread" because the area was a grain-producing region in Old Testament times. The name Ephrathah ("fruitful") differentiates it from the Galilean town by the same name. The town, known for its many vineyards and olive orchards, was small in size but not in honor.

FROM OF OLD, FROM EVERLASTING: This speaks of the eternal God's Incarnation in the person of Jesus Christ. It points to His millennial reign as King of kings (see Isaiah 9:6).

3. GIVE THEM UP: A reference to the interval between Messiah's rejection at His First Advent and His Second Advent, during the times of the Gentiles when Israel rejects Christ and is under the domination of enemies. Regathering of the "remnant of His brethren" did not occur at the First Advent but is slated for the Second Advent (see Isaiah 10:20–22; 11:11–16). Nor can "return" speak of Gentiles, since it cannot be said that they "returned" to the Lord. Rather, the context of verses 3–4 is millennial and cannot be made to fit the First Advent. Thus, "she who is in labor" must denote the nation of Israel (see Revelation 12:1–6).

4. HE SHALL STAND: The millennial rule of Christ, sitting upon the throne of David (see Isaiah 6:13).

5–6. ASSYRIAN: Assyria, God's instrument against Israel (722 BC) and Judah (Sennacherib's siege in 701 BC), is here used as representative of enemy nations in opposition to the Lord.

5. SEVEN . . . EIGHT: An idiom for a full and sufficient number of leaders, more than enough for the task (see Ecclesiastes 11:2).

6. NIMROD: A reference to Assyria (see Genesis 10:11) that could possibly also include Babylon (see Genesis 10:10).

7–9. MIDST OF MANY PEOPLES: Israel's presence in the midst of many peoples would be a source of blessing to some (see Zechariah 8:22–23), while to others, she would be like a lion—a source of fear and destruction (see Isaiah 11:14; Zechariah 12:2–3, 6; 14:14).

9. ALL YOUR ENEMIES: This absolute and complete peace has never yet been experienced by Israel. This points to the millennial kingdom when the Prince of Peace will reign, having conquered the nations (see verse 15).

10. IN THAT DAY: The future kingdom is in view. Israel had been forbidden the use of cavalry (see Deuteronomy 17:16), lest they trust in earthly forces rather than God (see 1 Kings 10:26, 28). God will remove all implements in which they

trust so that the people, stripped of all human resources, rest only in Him. War instruments will have no place in that time of peace.

11–14. CUT OFF THE CITIES . . . STRONGHOLDS: Continuing the thought from verse 10, fortified cities were designed for defense; their strength tempted people to put their trust in them rather than God alone (see Micah 1:13; Psalm 27:1; Hosea 10:13–14). People will live in peace in unwalled villages (see Ezekiel 38:11; Zechariah 2:4). The cities are also associated with centers of pagan worship (verse 14; see also Deuteronomy 16:21), the worship of Asherah (the Canaanite goddess of fertility and war). All forms of self-reliance in war and idolatrous worship will be removed so that the nation must rely solely on Christ their King for deliverance and worship Him alone.

UNLEASHING THE TEXT

1) The language in Micah 3:1–7 is intentionally graphic and shocking. What was Micah communicating through those verses to the leaders of Judah?

_____

_____

_____

_____

_____

_____

2) Micah's prophecy of the Lord's reign in Zion (4:1–5) points forward in time to the millennial kingdom, which will take place on earth after the Tribulation and the Second Coming of Christ. What passages reveal this general timeline?

_____

_____

_____

_____

_____

_____

_____

_____

3) What do you learn about the millennial kingdom based on Micah's words in chapter 4?

_____

_____

_____

_____

_____

_____

4) What are some promises that God makes to His people in Micah 5? How do those promises apply to believers in Christ today?

_____

_____

_____

_____

_____

_____

EXPLORING THE MEANING

Beware the Pitfalls of Power. Micah did not shy away from calling out the rulers, priests, and prophets of Israel—all of whom carried the responsibility of leading the people toward the Lord God (see 3:9–12). Authority and power are always coupled with responsibility. Those who have wealth should use that wealth to further God's kingdom. Those who are influential should use that influence to bring people closer to God. Those who believe in Jesus and have a relationship with Him should demonstrate the love of Christ to others through the example of their lives. We are each to use the gifts that we have received from God in service to Jesus, our rightful King, and not for our own self-interests. As Peter wrote, "As each one has received a gift, minister it to one another, as good stewards of the manifold grace of God" (1 Peter 4:10).

Remember the King Is Coming. Although Micah delivered a message of admonition to the rich and powerful of his day, he also delivered a prophecy of hope to the hurting, downcast, and downtrodden (see 4:1–5:5). This was a message of expectation and a promise of deliverance in the future. There would come a time when Jesus, the Messiah and the King of kings, would rule not only over the Jewish people but also over all the earth. As Micah wrote, "Many nations shall come and say, 'Come, and let us go up to the mountain of the LORD, to the house of the God of Jacob; He will teach us His ways, and we shall walk in His paths'" (4:2). Notice that the Millennium will be a time of peace and prosperity not only for nations in a general sense but also for every specific individual: "But everyone shall sit under his vine and under his fig tree, and no one shall make them afraid; for the mouth of the LORD of hosts has spoken" (4:4). The coming of the King will transform our world in radical and wonderful ways.

Recognize the Victory You Have in Christ. As we have seen, the situation for the "regular" people of Micah's day was bleak. God was preparing to judge Judah not only for the deceitfulness and idolatry of its leaders but also for their injustice and corruption. The wealthy and powerful had treated those beneath them cruelly—as if their fellow citizens were animals fit to be butchered (see 3:2–3)—and the priests and false prophets had spread a message of prosperity designed to further their own interests. Thankfully, Micah ends his second oracle with a more hopeful message. When God's people abandon their sinful ways and turn toward Him, they receive the promise that He will comfort them, protect them, and provide them with peace: "He shall stand and feed His flock in the strength of the LORD, in the majesty of the name of the LORD His God; and they shall abide, for now He shall be great to the ends of the earth; and this One shall be peace" (5:4–5). We need not put our faith in the protections of this world. We can trust solely in Jesus, the Messiah, who offers the only protection and safe harbor that we need.

REFLECTING ON THE TEXT

5) What were the characteristics of Israel's corrupt rulers? Are these characteristics common among the leaders and power brokers in our culture today?

---

6) What were the characteristics of Israel's false prophets? Are these characteristics common among the leaders of churches in general? What about the leaders and elders of the church that you attend?

_____
_____
_____
_____
_____
_____
_____

7) The Millennium will be defined by peace and prosperity to such a degree that people "shall beat their swords into plowshares, and their spears into pruning hooks" (Micah 4:3). In what ways do war and strife impact the world as a whole? What about in your life?

_____
_____
_____
_____
_____
_____
_____

8) What are some of the ways that our culture promises to protect its people? To what degree have those promises been fulfilled? How will the millennial kingdom compare?

_____
_____
_____
_____
_____
_____
_____

PERSONAL RESPONSE

9) To what degree are you listening to people who tell you what you *want* to hear rather than what you *need* to hear? Where can you turn for the latter?

_____

_____

_____

_____

_____

_____

_____

_____

10) What are some specific steps you can take to acknowledge Christ's sovereignty and authority over your life?

_____

_____

_____

_____

_____

_____

_____

3

GOD'S ULTIMATE DELIVERANCE
Micah 6:1–7:20

DRAWING NEAR

What have been some of the major landmarks or stages in your relationship with God?

_____

_____

_____

_____

_____

_____

_____

_____

_____

_____

_____

_____

_____

_____

_____

_____

_____

_____

_____

THE CONTEXT

There is a tradition that runs throughout the Old Testament of prophets and other representatives of God calling on the heavens and the earth to seve as witnesses between humanity and God—or as witnesses to the various covenants that were sealed between God and His people. For instance, in Deuteronomy 4:26, we read of Moses saying to the people, "I call heaven and earth to witness against you this day." He also called out to cosmic witnesses in Deuteronomy 32:1 while singing of God's faithfulness: "Give ear, O heavens, and I will speak; and hear, O earth, the words of my mouth." The function of these witnesses was to speak up when needed.

Micah's third oracle (6:1–7:20) follows in this biblical tradition. The prophet begins by relating these words from God: "Hear, O you mountains, the LORD's complaint, and you strong foundations of the earth; for the LORD has a complaint against His people" (6:2). The Lord here is calling on the mountains and foundations of the earth to testify about His faithfulness to His chosen people—and about the unfaithfulness of that same people in turning to idolatry.

However, as with Micah's other oracles, the third proclamation ends on a stirring note of hope for the future—including prophecies pertaining to both the millennial kingdom and other eras in which God will bless His people. Micah reveals that God will remain faithful to the covenants He made with Israel. A day will come when He completely fulfills His end of the bargain and blesses a future remnant of Abraham's offspring who turn back to Him.

KEYS TO THE TEXT

Read Micah 6:1–7:20, noting the key words and phrases indicated below.

> *MESSAGES OF REPROOF AND LAMENT: Micah opens the third cycle of oracles with another dramatic courtroom motif that moves back and forth between three speakers: (1) the Lord pleading His case, (2) the people responding under conviction, (3) and the prophet as the lawyer for the plaintiff.*

6:1–2. MOUNTAINS . . . HILLS: The Lord commanded Micah (verse 1), as His advocate, to plead His case before the mountains and hills, which were to act as witnesses against His people (see Deuteronomy 4:25–26; Isaiah 1:2). The mountains and hills were present at Sinai when the Lord made His covenant with

Israel and when the commandments were written and placed in the ark of the covenant as a permanent witness (see Deuteronomy 31:26).

3–5. WHAT HAVE I DONE TO YOU: This was the Lord's appeal. With tenderness and emotion, the divine Plaintiff recalled His many gracious acts toward them, almost to the point of assuming the tone of a defendant. Noting their trek from bondage in Egypt to their own homeland, God had provided leadership (verse 4), reversed the attempts of Balaam to curse the people (verse 5a; see also Numbers 22–24), and miraculously parted the Jordan River (verse 5b) so they could cross over from Acacia Grove, located east of the Jordan, to Gilgal on the west side near Jericho. God had faithfully kept all His promises to them.

6–7. WITH WHAT SHALL I COME BEFORE THE LORD: Micah, as though speaking on behalf of the people, asked rhetorically how, in light of God's faithfulness toward them, they could continue their hypocrisy by being outwardly religious but inwardly sinful.

8. WHAT DOES THE LORD REQUIRE OF YOU: Micah's terse response in this verse indicates that the people should have known the answer to the rhetorical question. Spiritual blindness had led them to offer everything except the one thing God wanted—a spiritual commitment of the heart from which right behavior would ensue (see Deuteronomy 10:12–19; Matthew 22:37–39). This theme is often represented in the Old Testament (see 1 Samuel 15:22; Isaiah 1:11–20; Jeremiah 7:21–23; Hosea 6:6; Amos 5:15).

9–16. THE LORD'S VOICE CRIES: The Lord was sending judgment; God Himself had appointed the "rod" that would punish them. The Lord spoke, noting that their corrupt deeds perpetrated on the poor were still continuing in spite of His warnings and discipline (verses 10–12). Therefore, a severe judgment was coming (verses 13–15); it would happen to them just as it did to their northern neighbor, Israel (verse 16), when led by the counsel of wicked kings.

9. HEAR THE ROD: They were to listen for the description of the coming punishment (see verses 13–15; Isaiah 10:5, 24).

16. STATUTES OF OMRI: Circa 885–874 BC. Omri was the founder of Samaria and of Ahab's wicked house, as well as a supporter of Jeroboam's superstitions (see 1 Kings 16:16–28).

WORKS OF AHAB'S HOUSE: See 1 Kings 21:25–26 (c. 874–853 BC).

7:1–6. WOE IS ME: Micah sounded like Isaiah (see Isaiah 6:5), lamenting the circumstances of his day. In his vain search for an upright person (verse 2), he compared himself to the vinedresser who enters his vineyard late in the season and finds no fruit. The leaders conspired together to get what they wanted (verse 3). No one could be trusted (verses 5–6). Christ would later use verse 6 as an illustration when He commissioned the Twelve (see Matthew 10:1, 35–36).

> MESSAGES OF CONFIDENCE AND VICTORY: *Micah, in spite of his dire circumstances, as a watchman (see verse 4) would intently look for evidence of God's working, trusting God to act in His own time and His own way (see Habakkuk 3:16–19).*

8–10. I WILL ARISE: Micah depicts Israel confessing her faith in the Lord, warning her enemies she would rise again (verses 8, 10). She confesses her sin, acknowledging the justice of God's punishment and anticipating His restoration.

10. WHERE IS THE LORD YOUR GOD: See Psalm 42:3, 10; Matthew 27:43.

11–13. IN THE DAY . . . THAT DAY: Micah again spoke, recounting the blessings awaiting the faithful remnant in Messiah's millennial rule. It would include unprecedented expansion (see Zechariah 2:1–5) and a massive infusion of immigrants (see Isaiah 11:15–16). For those who defied Messiah's millennial rulership, their land would become desolate (verse 13; see also Zechariah 14:16–19).

14–17. SHEPHERD YOUR PEOPLE: Micah petitioned the Lord to shepherd, feed, and protect His people like a flock (see Psalm 23). The Lord answered, reiterating that He would demonstrate His presence and power among them as He did in the Exodus from Egypt (verse 15). As a result, the vaunted pride and power of the nations would be rendered powerless (see Joshua 2:9–11) and, having been humbled (verse 17), they would no longer listen to or engage in the taunting of His people (verse 16b; see also Genesis 12:3; Isaiah 52:15).

15. WONDERS: These miracles will be fulfilled in God's judgment on the earth that precedes the Second Advent of Messiah (see Revelation 6–19).

18–20. WHO IS A GOD LIKE YOU: Micah, whose name means "Who is like the Lord," begins his concluding thoughts with a play on words involving his name. In response to the gracious, forgiving character displayed toward Israel by their Master, the repentant remnant of the people extolled His incomparable grace and mercy (see Psalm 130:3–4).

20. SWORN TO OUR FATHERS: In spite of Israel's unfaithfulness, the Lord intended to fulfill His unconditional promises in the Abrahamic covenant made with Abraham and confirmed with Isaac and Jacob (see Genesis 12; 15; 17; 22; 26; 28; 35). When enacted in conjunction with the Davidic covenant, Israel will again

be restored as a people and a nation to the land originally promised to Abraham. Jesus Christ, the ultimate descendant of David, will rule from Jerusalem over the world as King of kings and Lord of lords (see Revelation 17:14; 19:16).

UNLEASHING THE TEXT

1) Summarize the "case" that God makes against His people in Micah 6:1–8.

_____

_____

_____

_____

_____

2) Micah 6:8 is a well-known and well-loved verse. What exactly does it mean to "do justly," to "love mercy," and to "walk humbly" with God? On a practial level, what does that look like?

_____

_____

_____

_____

_____

_____

3) What reasons did the prophet have for "woe" as expressed in Micah 7:1–7?

_____

_____

_____

_____

_____

4) What reasons did the prophet have for hope as expressed in Micah 7:8–20?

_____

_____

_____

_____

_____

EXPLORING THE MEANING

Remember What God Has Done in the Past. We live in such a fast-paced world that it can be easy for us to forget to pause at times and reflect on where God has been present in our lives. If we are not careful, we can get so caught up with the pressing issues of the moment that we miss out on all the ways that God is leading us through difficult situations and preparing the way forward for our future. At the beginning of Micah 6, God implored Judah to do just that—to remember how He had been with them and provided for them, even when their hearts were hard toward Him. "For I brought you up from the land of Egypt, I redeemed you from the house of bondage. . . . O My people, remember now" (verses 4–5). This was a key moment in Micah's prophecy. If the people had stopped and listened— if they had repented and acknowledged God's sovereignty—He would have shown compassion. But instead they chose to continue down the wrong path. When faced with the same choice, how will we respond?

Remember the Hope That God Provides. The book of Micah, like many of the prophetic books in the Bible, can seem heavy at times. The people of Judah had turned away from the Lord and were following after other gods. They had forgotten God's acts of faithfulness in the past and were choosing to be unfaithful to Him. God was now calling them to account for their actions and pronouncing His judgments against them. "Therefore I will also make you sick by striking you, by making you desolate because of your sins. . . . And what you do rescue I will give over to the sword" (Micah 6:13–14). Yet even in spite of these judgments, Micah could offer his people hope: "[The Lord] does not retain His anger forever, because He delights in mercy. He will again have compassion on us, and will subdue our iniquities" (7:18–19). Micah reminds us of the hope that even though there are consequences for sin, our heavenly Father delights in mercy, and He will extend His compassion and forgiveness to us when we repent of our sins.

Remember That God Always Keeps His Promises. The greatest promise in the Old Testament is that God would send a Savior to take away the sins of His people and bring Creation back to the glory and purpose He intended from the beginning. As He promised to Abraham, "I will bless those who bless you, and I will curse him who curses you; and in you all the families of the earth shall be blessed" (Genesis 12:3). Micah's prophecy ends with a description of a messianic age ruled by the Savior sent from God to defeat Satan. Now, because of Christ, our sins have been pardoned and our tears wiped away, so that we might say, like Micah, "Who is a God like You, pardoning iniquity and passing over the transgression of the remnant of His heritage? He does not retain His anger forever, because He delights in mercy" (7:18).

REFLECTING ON THE TEXT

5) Why is it often so easy to forget some of the ways that God has been faithful to you in the past? What are some specific acts of God's faithfulness that you can recall right now?

_____

_____

_____

_____

_____

_____

6) In spite of God sending many prophets to compel His people to turn away from their sins, they ultimately persisted in their idolatry. How would the story of God's people have ended differently if they had truly repented?

_____

_____

_____

_____

_____

_____

7) Based on the book of Micah, what are some of the reasons that you can put your hope in Christ?

_____

_____

_____

_____

_____

_____

8) God always delivers on His promises. What are some specific promises mentioned in Micah that are particularly encouraging to believers today?

_____

_____

_____

_____

_____

PERSONAL RESPONSE

9) "Do justly . . . love mercy . . . walk humbly with your God" (Micah 6:8). What opportunites do you have this week to obey these commands? Be specific.

_____

_____

_____

_____

_____

10) What have you appreciated most from your study of the book of Micah? Why did those particular aspects of the book stand out to you?

_____

_____

_____

_____

_____

4

GOD'S JUDGMENT ON JUDAH
Zephaniah 1:1–2:3

DRAWING NEAR

What are some ways your parents and grandparents have influenced your spiritual life? What are some of the biggest lessons that they taught you?

_____

_____

_____

_____

_____

_____

_____

_____

_____

_____

_____

_____

_____

_____

_____

_____

_____

_____

_____

_____

_____

_____

_____

THE CONTEXT

After the reign of King Solomon (c. 971–931 BC), what had been known as the united nation of Israel was divided into two separate kingdoms. The northern kingdom became known as Israel, and its capital was Samaria. The southern kingdom was called Judah, and its capital was Jerusalem. All nineteen of the kings who ruled over the northern kingdom were evil, leading the people away from God and toward idolatry. Twelve out of the twenty kings who ruled over Judah were wicked as well. Only eight kings tried to steer the people of Judah back to the faith of David and Solomon.

Zephaniah was a prophet in the southern kingdom. He ministered primarily during the reign of a godly king named Josiah (c. 640–609 BC), who took the throne at the young age of eight. However, Josiah's father (Amon) and grandfather (Manasseh) had been ungodly kings who had led Judah into spiritual darkness for more than five decades (c. 695–640 BC). Zephaniah and other faithful prophets (including Jeremiah) spoke often of the consequences the people were about to experience because of their prolonged rebellion and idolatry.

As you will discover in this lesson, the primary theme of Zephaniah follows a similar template to the other prophetic books. Judgment is declared against Judah, along with many other nations. Specifically, God would judge Judah and Jerusalem through oppression and eventual conquest at the hands of King Nebuchadnezzar and the armies of Babylon. Even so, many of Zephaniah's prophetic words point forward to the hope of a future restoration.

KEYS TO THE TEXT

Read Zephaniah 1:1–2:3, noting the key words and phrases indicated below.

> *THE LORD'S JUDGMENT ON THE WHOLE EARTH: Zephaniah begins by noting the far fulfillment of the Day of the Lord, when even animals and physical creation will be affected by God's judgment of the earth.*

1:1. HEZEKIAH . . . JOSIAH: Zephaniah traced his royal lineage back to his great-great-grandfather Hezekiah (c. 715–686 BC) and placed his ministry contemporaneous with Josiah (c. 640–609 BC).

2. FACE OF THE LAND: Generally translated "ground," the term is used in reference to the whole earth (see Zephaniah 1:18). The phraseology is reminiscent of the Noahic Flood (see Genesis 6:7, 17; 7:21–23).

3. I WILL CONSUME: Comparisons with the Genesis Flood continue with "man and beast" and "birds of the heavens" (see Genesis 6:7; 7:23). The prophet also alluded to the creation, pairing man and beast (sixth day of creation) and birds with fish (fifth day of creation).

STUMBLING BLOCKS: Whatever alienates man from God will be removed.

THE LORD'S JUDGMENT ON JUDAH: The Lord narrows His words *of judgment to focus specifically on Judah, specifying the causes of judgment as apostasy and idolatry, which are always coupled with moral and ethical corruption.*

4. CUT OFF EVERY TRACE OF BAAL: The worship of Baal, the Canaanite god of fertility, was a constant source of temptation to Israel (see Numbers 25:1–5; Judges 2:13), as the people tried to worship him alongside the worship of the Lord (see Jeremiah 7:9; 23:25–29). This mix became a primary cause for judgment (see 2 Kings 17:16–20; Jeremiah 11:13–17; Hosea 2:8), which would forever excise the worship of Baal from Israel.

5. WORSHIP THE HOST OF HEAVEN: Astrology was also a prominent part of Israel's idolatrous practices; they worshiped the host of heaven from as early as the Exodus (see Deuteronomy 4:19; Amos 5:25–26; Acts 7:40–43). God warned them repeatedly, but they rebelled (see 2 Kings 23:5–6; Jeremiah 7:17–18; 8:2; 44:17–25). Altars were often erected on housetop roofs to provide a clear view of the sky (see Jeremiah 8:2; 19:13; 32:29).

SWEAR BY MILCOM: Judah's syncretistic worship was reflected in the practice of swearing by the Lord and, at the same time, by Milcom. This god may have either been the Ammonite deity mentioned in 1 Kings 11:5, 33 or Molech, the worship of whom included child sacrifice, astrology, and temple prostitution (see Leviticus 18:21; 2 Kings 17:16–17; Ezekiel 23:37; Amos 5:25–26; Acts 7:40–43).

6. WHO HAVE TURNED BACK: Zephaniah concluded with those who had at first heeded calls to repentance but later had willfully turned away.

7. BE SILENT: In view of God's just judgment, there was no defense to be spoken and, in view of the devastation, only shocked and mute wonder (see Habakkuk 2:20; Zechariah 2:13).

DAY OF THE LORD: See notes on Joel 1:15.

PREPARED A SACRIFICE . . . INVITED HIS GUESTS: God's judgment on Israel was viewed as His sacrifice. The guests were the dreaded Babylonians, who as "priests" were invited to kill the sacrifice; that is, Judah (see Isaiah 13:3; 34:6; Jeremiah 46:10; Ezekiel 39:17; Habakkuk 1:6; Revelation 19:17–18).

8. THE PRINCES ... KING'S CHILDREN: Judgment began with the royal house. Lacking commitment to God's covenant, they had adopted the customs and idolatrous practices of the heathen. Josiah was only eight years old when he assumed rulership, so the reference would not be to his children but to the princes of the royal house or to the children of the king who would be ruling when the prophecy was fulfilled (see 2 Kings 25:7; Jeremiah 39:6).

9. LEAP OVER THE THRESHOLD: This describes the eagerness with which the rich hurried from their homes to plunder the poor.

10–11. FISH GATE ... SECOND QUARTER ... MAKTESH: The merchants, made wealthy from dishonest gain (see verse 9), were singled out to depict the anguish of the coming judgment. The Fish Gate, known today as the Damascus Gate, was located on the north side. The Second Quarter was a district within the city walls. Maktesh, meaning "mortar," was a name applied to the Valley of Siloam because of its shape; it was a district where merchants carried on business.

12. I WILL SEARCH: None would escape the punishment of the Lord (see Amos 9:1–4).

SETTLED IN COMPLACENCY: The prophet used this term, which refers to a thickened crust that forms on wine when left undisturbed for a long period of time, to describe the people's indifference and slothfulness toward God. Their indifference led them to regard God as morally indifferent.

14–18. IS NEAR AND HASTENS QUICKLY: Zephaniah vividly describes the Day of the Lord in staccato fashion, rehearsing the ominous conditions characterizing that day. This section seems to point to a near fulfillment when Babylon subdued Judah (see verses 4–13) as well as the ultimate far fulfillment that will involve the whole earth (verse 18).

16. DAY OF TRUMPET AND ALARM: In accordance with God's instructions, a trumpet was fashioned for the purpose of sounding an alarm (see Numbers 10:1–10).

17–18. BLOOD . . . LIKE DUST: As though worthless, their blood and flesh would be discarded as dust. Their silver and gold, corruptly gained (see verses 9–13), would be of no avail to protect them from the wrath of holy God (see Jeremiah 46:28).

17. WALK LIKE BLIND MEN: As blind men, they would grope unsuccessfully for escape routes (see Deuteronomy 28:29).

18. THE WHOLE LAND SHALL BE DEVOURED: The discussion now expands to include the whole earth, as in verses 2–3.

> A CALL TO REPENTANCE: *Following this announcement of coming judgment, God mercifully invites His people to repent. They are to assemble in order to entreat the favor of the Lord and avert His wrath.*

2:1. UNDESIRABLE NATION: The people of Judah, no longer sensitive to God's call to repentance through His many prophets, had sunk to shamelessness.

3. IT MAY BE THAT YOU WILL BE HIDDEN: Even the meek—those who had followed the law of the Lord—were encouraged to continue to show fruits of repentance so they would be sheltered in the day of His judgment (see Isaiah 26:20).

UNLEASHING THE TEXT

1) What are some striking phrases or images in Zephaniah 1? What do those phrases and images reveal?

_____

_____

_____

_____

_____

_____

2) What does Zephaniah 1:4–6 teach about the spiritual condition of Judah?

_____

_____

_____

_____

_____

3) What is the "sacrifice" that the Lord says He has prepared in Zephaniah 1:8?

_____

_____

_____

_____

_____

4) How does Zephaniah 1:14–16 describe the Day of the Lord?

_____

_____

_____

_____

EXPLORING THE MEANING

The Time to Repent Is Now. The apostle Peter wrote, "The Lord is not slack concerning His promise, as some count slackness, but is longsuffering toward us, not willing that any should perish but that all should come to repentance" (2 Peter 3:9). God had been patient with Judah. He had sent His prophets to warn the people of what would happen if they did not turn from their sins. But the people had persisted in their idolatry, and now God's judgment was about to fall on them. Zephaniah's message to the people was thus, "The time to repent is now!" The same is true in our lives. God convicts us of our sins and gives us the opportunity to repent. But we need to recognize that He is being merciful and not delay in confessing our transgressions.

God Cares About People's Sin. God revealed to Zephaniah that He was coming to "punish the men who are settled in complacency, who say in their heart, 'The LORD will not do good, nor will He do evil'" (1:12). These individuals had evidently developed an attitude of indifference toward God and had wrongly concluded that He would be likewise be indifferent toward their sin. However, as the psalmist said of the Lord, "You are not a God who takes pleasure in wickedness, nor shall evil dwell with You" (Psalm 5:4). We may think that God turns a blind eye to our sin, but the reality is that it matters to Him how we choose to live our lives. He truly desires us to "seek first the kingdom of God and His righteousness" (Matthew 6:33).

God Responds to Repentance. Zephaniah was very much an "eleventh-hour" prophet to the nation of Judah. By the time he appeared on the scene during the early reign of Josiah, the kingdom had endured some fifty-five years of ungodly rule at the hands of Josiah's grandfather (Manasseh) and father (Amon). The corruption and idolatry in Judah ran deep, yet as we discover in Zephaniah 2:1–3, the Lord still longed for His people to repent and return to Him. What is unusual in Zephaniah's case is that King Josiah *did* actually enact reforms that led the people back to the true worship of the Lord. As a result, God paused on enacting His judgment. This reveals that God will respond with mercy to those who choose the path of righteousness. Truly, as Zephaniah prophesied, they will "be hidden in the day of the LORD's anger" (verse 3).

REFLECTING ON THE TEXT

5) What will Judah say concerning the Day of the Lord, according to verse 12? What does our culture say about God's future global judgment?

_____

_____

_____

_____

_____

6) What is our culture's approach to spiritual morality? How does it compare to Judah's approach in Zephaniah? What is God's approach to spiritual morality as recorded in the pages of Scripture?

_____

_____

_____

_____

_____

_____

7) What does it mean to be complacent in your faith? Why did God state in Zephaniah 1:12 that He would punish those who were "settled in complacency"?

_____

_____

_____

_____

_____

_____

8) What counsel was Judah given in light of the coming Day of the Lord? Is this counsel applicable to everyone?

_____

_____

_____

_____

_____

_____

PERSONAL RESPONSE

9) What steps do you take in a typical week to expose yourself to God's truth as revealed in His Word? What additional steps would you like to take?

_____

_____

_____

_____

_____

_____

10) Who are some people you can give permission to tell you when you have become spiritually complacent? What steps will you take to reach out to those people this week?

_____

_____

_____

_____

_____

_____

5

GOD'S JUDGMENT ON THE NATIONS
Zephaniah 2:4–3:20

DRAWING NEAR

What are some of the countries that have been in the news in recent weeks? What do you know about the spiritual condition of those nations?

_____

_____

_____

_____

_____

_____

_____

_____

_____

_____

_____

_____

_____

_____

_____

_____

_____

_____

_____

_____

THE CONTEXT

Most cultures and religious expressions in the ancient world were what we might call "local." Each nation or people group developed its own particular system of gods, with the idea that those deities held geographical connections. Certain gods were connected with certain mountains, for example, and worshiped in the high places. Other regions worshiped gods connected with specific rivers, plains, and so on. Importantly, clashes between nations and armies were viewed as clashes between regional gods—with the stronger gods proving themselves to be victorious through the strength of the armies that worshiped them.

It is important to keep this context in mind as you read through Zephaniah's proclamations of judgment against various regions, nations, and people groups in this next portion of his prophecy. The God of Israel was not like the other would-be gods whom the people in the ancient world worshiped. He was not limited to Mount Zion or the hills of Palestine. Instead, the Lord God claimed authority over *all* nations and peoples.

You can see that authority in Zephaniah 2–3 in the way that God rendered judgment on the foreign peoples who did not worship Him. You can also see that authority in the way He rendered judgment on the people of Judah and Jerusalem who did worship Him. In both cases, God set Himself apart as Judge over all the earth.

KEYS TO THE TEXT

Read Zephaniah 2:4–3:20, noting the key words and phrases indicated below.

> PUNISHMENT OF NATIONS: *God would use heathen nations to punish His people, but He would not permit those nations to go unpunished. To illustrate this, four representative nations are chosen from the four points of the compass.*

2:4–7. GAZA . . . EKRON: The first nation to be judged was Philistia, located to the west of Israel. Judgment was to come swiftly and unexpectedly, even at noonday when it was least expected. Of the five Philistine cities, only Gath was omitted (see Amos 1:6–8).

5. CHERETHITES: Occasionally a synonym for Philistia, this term represented a branch from Crete. David's bodyguard was comprised of both Cherethites and Pelethites (see 2 Samuel 8:18; 1 Kings 1:38, 44).

7. RETURN THEIR CAPTIVES: The Lord would initiate the physical return of Israel's exiles to occupy the land vacated by judgment on Philistia.

8–11. MOAB . . . AMMON: Located to the east of Israel, these descendants of Lot by his daughters through incest (see Genesis 19:30–38) had reproached and reviled God's people, incurring His divine wrath (see Genesis 12:3). Like Sodom and Gomorrah in the days of their ancestor Lot, they too would come to ruin and desolation.

11. WORSHIP HIM . . . ALL THE SHORES OF THE NATIONS: The final fulfillment of these predictions is yet future, depicting the Millennium when all the gods of the nations will be reduced to nothing and the Lord Himself will be worshiped universally (see Isaiah 66:18–21; Zechariah 14:16; Malachi 1:11).

12. ETHIOPIA: Located to the south of Israel, she would be judged by God's sword. This was fulfilled in Nebuchadnezzar's invasion and conquest of Egypt (see Ezekiel 30:24–25).

13–15. ASSYRIA . . . NINEVEH: Assyria, located northwest of Israel, would be desolated as well. Nineveh, the Assyrian capital, fell shortly after this prophecy to the Babylonians in 612 BC. Famed for her irrigation system, she would be left dry.

15. THAT SAID IN HER HEART: In language similar to that of the king of Babylon (see Isaiah 14:13–14; 47:8) and the prince of Tyre (see Ezekiel 28:2), Assyria had claimed divine attributes for herself. For this, she would be brought to ruin.

> WOE ON JERUSALEM: *After pronouncing judgment on the nations, the prophet returns again to pronouncing woe upon Jerusalem. Because of that city's favored position among the nations (see Exodus 19:5), more obedience was expected; thus, there was greater punishment for her disobedience.*

3:2. SHE HAS NOT RECEIVED CORRECTION: Jerusalem was soon to learn that to reject God's correction leads to destruction (see Proverbs 5:23).

SHE HAS NOT DRAWN NEAR TO HER GOD: The Lord had taken up residence in that city, making Him easily accessible (see Deuteronomy 4:7), yet they had refused to draw near to Him in proper worship.

3–5. HER PRINCES . . . HER JUDGES . . . HER PROPHETS . . . HER PRIESTS: Four classes of leadership were singled out for condemnation. The political leaders— the (1) princes and (2) judges—were both likened to ravenous wolves, endlessly searching for more prey (see Zephaniah 1:8–9). The spiritual leaders—the (3) prophets and (4) priests—were unfaithful to the Lord whom they claimed to represent. By contrast, the Lord never failed to manifest a faithful standard of justice and righteousness.

6–7. BUT THEY ROSE EARLY: The desolations brought by the Lord on surrounding nations were to serve as warnings to Judah, meant to turn His people back to Him. Instead, enticed by the fruits of corruption, the people rose early to zealously and deliberately pursue the way of sin.

8. THE DAY I RISE UP: The prophet here transitions from the historical invasion of Judah by Babylon to the future Day of the Lord. He speaks of the Great Tribulation, when the Lord will gather all the nations for judgment (see Joel 3:1–2, 12–17; Zechariah 12:2–3; 14:2; Matthew 24:21). The faithful remnant, presumably the meek of Zephaniah 2:1–3, are exhorted to wait in trust for Him to carry out His judgment.

THE LORD'S BLESSING: The final section of Zephaniah's prophecy unveils the blessings of restoration for God's people and the nations.

9. PURE LANGUAGE: A remnant of the nations, converted to the Lord, will worship Him in righteousness and truth (see Zechariah 8:20–23; 14:16). Pure speech will come from purified hearts (see Luke 6:45).

10. BEYOND THE RIVERS OF ETHIOPIA: They will return from distant places (see Isaiah 11:11, 15–16; 27:13).

11–13. NO LONGER BE HAUGHTY: The Lord will purge the proud and ungodly from among them (see Zechariah 13:1–6), leaving a meek and humble people. Material prosperity and peace will accompany them as well, allowing them to enjoy the rich blessings of God undisturbed (see Joel 3:18–20; Micah 4:4).

14–20. SING, O DAUGHTER OF ZION: The messianic era of millennial blessing and restoration is described.

15–17. TAKEN AWAY YOUR JUDGMENTS: The basis for rejoicing in verse 14 is that Israel's day of judgment is past and her King is residing in her midst. His departure just prior to Nebuchadnezzar's destruction of the temple is graphically depicted in Ezekiel 8–11, but He will return as Lord and Messiah, a fact so glorious that it is repeated in verse 17.

17. REJOICE OVER YOU: As a bridegroom rejoices over his bride (see Isaiah 62:4), so the Lord will exult over His people with gladness and song, resting

in quiet ecstasy over His people in whom is His delight (see Deuteronomy 30:9; Isaiah 54:1–17).

18. THOSE WHO SORROW OVER THE APPOINTED ASSEMBLY: The godly remnant will sorrow because they are unable to celebrate the appointed feasts (see Exodus 23:14–17). But the Lord will remove their sorrow, giving them praise and fame (see verse 19).

19–20. AT THAT TIME: The time of Messiah's return, when the Jews will be regathered and become a source of blessing to the world, fulfilling Israel's original destiny (see Deuteronomy 26:18–19; Isaiah 62:7).

UNLEASHING THE TEXT

1) What are some of the nations that God selects for punishment in Zephaniah 2:4–15? What stands out to you about the nature of these judgments?

_____

_____

_____

_____

_____

2) Put yourself in the place of those in Jerusalem who heard Zephaniah's prophecy. How might they have responded to these proclamations of judgment against the nations?

_____

_____

_____

_____

3) Jerusalem would not be spared from God's judgment. What claims did God make about them (see 3:1–7)? What are some similarities between that culture and our culture?

_____

_____

_____

_____

4) God made several promises in Zephaniah 3:8–20 regarding His chosen people. Which of those promises have been fulfilled? Which are yet to be fulfilled?

_____

_____

_____

_____

EXPLORING THE MEANING

God's Justice Reaches Every Corner of the World. It can often seem that those who willfully oppose God—who do evil in His sight and commit transgressions against Him—just get away with it. Thankfully, this is not true. In Zephaniah 2:4–15, God revealed His authority to judge _all_ the nations of the world for their sins against His people. What is interesting is that these prophecies were not directed to the offending nations but were meant for the ears of the Jewish people. In other words, God was letting His children know that He will not allow such evil to go unpunished. Although God is patient, He will eventually mete out His judgment on all who forsake Him or turn their backs on Him. Zephaniah's words helped the Jewish people understand that God's justice was inevitable. It might not occur when they wanted it or expected it, but the Lord _would_ bring justice to every corner of the world.

God's People Are to Be an Example to the World. God's justice was not reserved only for the foreign nations. In Zephaniah 3, the prophet also proclaimed the Lord's judgments against the people of Jerusalem. God's people had been called to live as witnesses of His goodness and love to the world—to bless "all the families of the earth" (Genesis 12:3). The Lord considered them His "special treasure . . . above all people" (Exodus 19:5). They had been given a favored position among the nations—and thus He expected more obedience from them. Yet time and again, the people failed in this mission and chose to worship the gods of the foreign nations. As followers of Jesus, we are likewise "a chosen generation" (1 Peter 2:9). We have been called to be "the light of the world" (Matthew 5:14). Will we accept this mission and be "ambassadors for Christ" (2 Corinthians 5:20)? Or will we just blend in and be like the rest of the world?

God's Mercy Extends to Every Corner of the World. God is compassionate, full of mercy, and ready to forgive. When we turn to Him in repentance and put our faith in the saving work of Christ, we are given the promise that we will "not perish but have everlasting life" (John 3:16). Zephaniah concluded his prophecy with a glimpse of this glorious future that God has in store for His people—a day when Jesus will reign over the entire world. In that age, which will last for 1,000 years, He will bring order, prosperity, and peace to all people, including the nation of Israel. "In that day it shall be said to Jerusalem: 'Do not fear; Zion, let not your hands be weak. The LORD your God in your midst, the Mighty One, will save; He will rejoice over you with gladness, He will quiet you with His love, He will rejoice over you with singing'" (Zephaniah 3:16–17). These blessings are not only for the future remnant of Israel. Rather, God will create a worldwide season of bliss for "all nations, tribes, peoples, and tongues" (Revelation 7:9).

REFLECTING ON THE TEXT

5) What is the biblical definition of justice? What does it mean on a practical level?

_____

_____

_____

_____

_____

6) What are some ways God delivers justice in our world? What about in our lives?

_____

_____

_____

_____

_____

7) God intended the Israelites to be an example of His love and goodness to the world. As His chosen people, they were to reveal Him to all people. In a similar way, followers of Jesus are ambassadors of Christ. What does it mean to represent Jesus in our culture?

_____

_____

_____

_____

_____

8) Zephaniah ends with a glimpse of the future that God has planned for His people. What does this incredible future entail?

_____

_____

_____

_____

_____

PERSONAL RESPONSE

9) In what ways do you have an opportunity to be a representative of God's justice? How can you contribute to the outworking of God's justice in your community?

_____

_____

_____

_____

_____

10) In a similar way, where do you have an opportunity this week to take full advantage of your status as an ambassador for Christ? Be specific in your response.

_____

_____

_____

_____

_____

6

THE DESTRUCTION OF NINEVEH
Nahum 1:1–3:19

DRAWING NEAR
Use the space below to list a few of the most impressive cities that you have visited during your lifetime. What did you enjoy about each place?

_____

_____

_____

_____

_____

_____

_____

_____

_____

_____

_____

_____

_____

_____

_____

_____

_____

_____

_____

_____

THE CONTEXT

The history between Israel and Assyria is long and complex. As an ancient empire, the Assyrians were a dominant force in the region. Modern historians typically divide the empire into different periods: Early Assyrian (c. 2600–2025 BC), Old Assyrian (c. 2025–1364 BC), Middle Assyrian (c. 1363–912 BC), and Neo-Assyrian (911–609 BC). The influence of Assyria in Israel was kept at bay by the strength of David and Solomon (c. 1011–931 BC), but that strength quickly faded after Israel was divided into its northern and southern kingdoms.

It was around 760 BC when God said to Jonah, "Arise, go to Nineveh, that great city, and cry out against it; for their wickedness has come up before Me" (Jonah 1:2). Jonah eventually followed God's instruction to preach in Nineveh, the Assyrian capital, which led to a revival. However, forty years later, the Assyrians conquered the northern tribe of Israel and took many of its residents away as captives. In 701 BC, the Assyrian king Sennacherib tried to besiege Jerusalem, though his efforts were thwarted by divine intervention (see 2 Kings 8:13–19:37).

The prophecy of Nahum is unique in the Bible because it is addressed not to God's people in Israel or Judah but to the residents of Nineveh. Nahum's prophecy specifically and graphically sets forth doom against both Nineveh and the Assyrian Empire—and not just any doom, but God's judgment. Nahum's prophecies were fulfilled to the letter when a coalition led by Babylon defeated Assyria and destroyed Nineveh in 612 BC.

KEYS TO THE TEXT

Read Nahum 1:1–3:19, noting the key words and phrases indicated below.

> DESTRUCTION OF NINEVEH DECLARED: *Nahum introduces his prophecy as a "burden against Nineveh" (verse 1) because it is a message of doom.*

1:1. BURDEN: A weighty, heavy oracle of judgment is often depicted by this term when employed by prophets to announce God's wrath against sin (see Isaiah 13:1; 15:1; 17:1; 19:1; Habakkuk 1:1; Zechariah 9:1; 12:1; Malachi 1:1).

2–8. GOD IS JEALOUS: Nahum, defining God's power in general, establishes the fact that He is omnipotent: a holy and jealous God who will punish the wicked and avenge His own. The term "jealous"—often used of God's burning zeal for His wife, Israel—emphasizes His passionate reaction against anyone guilty of spiritual adultery. Possibly, the captivity of the ten northern tribes in 722 BC or the invasion of Sennacherib in 701 BC is in view here.

3. SLOW TO ANGER: The fact that "God is jealous" (verse 2) should not suggest that He is quick to anger; rather, He is longsuffering (see Exodus 34:6; Numbers 14:18). God had extended His forbearance to Nineveh at least a century earlier in response to their repentance at Jonah's preaching (see Jonah 3:10; 4:2). But although patient, His justice will eventually punish the wicked.

WHIRLWIND . . . STORM . . . CLOUDS: These figures frequently describe the Lord's appearances (theophanies), often in judgment (see Exodus 19:9, 16; Psalm 83:15; Isaiah 29:6; Joel 2:2; 1 Thessalonians 4:17). Nature serves as the theater in which His power and majesty are showcased.

4. HE REBUKES THE SEA: God's mighty power is revealed when He rebukes the sea, as in the crossing of the Red Sea (see Exodus 14:15–25), and when He withholds His rain from the fertile valleys and coastal highlands.

BASHAN: Bashan, located below Mount Hermon, east of the Jordan River, was known for her lush pastures (see Micah 7:14).

CARMEL: Carmel, located along the coast of Canaan, became synonymous with fruitfulness (see Song of Solomon 7:5).

LEBANON: Lebanon was renowned for her beautiful cedars (see 1 Kings 5:14–18), yet they too would wither before the infinite strength of the omnipotent Judge.

5. THE MOUNTAINS QUAKE . . . HILLS MELT: The violent shaking of the earth provides another evidence of the Lord's awesome power, as that which seems to be most stable trembles.

6. WHO CAN STAND . . . WHO CAN ENDURE: This series of rhetorical questions summarizes verses 2–5. God's power and resolve to spew His wrath on Nineveh is irresistible, melting all opposition before it.

7. THE LORD IS GOOD, A STRONGHOLD: In contrast to verse 6, Nahum eases the fury by adding that God is compassionate, a mighty fortress (see Psalm 46:1), to those who put their hope in Him (see Isaiah 33:2–4; 37:3–7, 29–38). The verse foreshadows the vindication of Judah in verses 12b–13, 15; 2:2.

8. AN OVERFLOWING FLOOD . . . AND DARKNESS: Nahum describes Nineveh's actual judgment metaphorically as an engulfing flood and darkness from which none can escape.

9–15. WHAT DO YOU CONSPIRE AGAINST THE LORD: Having now established God's power and sovereign right to judge in general, Nahum announces specifically God's judgment upon Nineveh, interweaving expressions of blessing and hope for Israel within the oracles of doom upon the wicked nation. The sovereign Judge not only punishes (verses 9–12a, 14) but also saves (verses 12b, 13, 15). All Assyrian attempts to "conspire against the LORD" (verse 9) or foil God's judgment would end in futility (see Psalm 2). The Ninevites' affliction of His people would not be allowed to occur again (see verse 12). Their end was determined.

11. WICKED COUNSELOR: This phrase, literally "counselor of Belial," suggests satanic influence on the leadership, identified as the king of Assyria (see Nahum 3:18). Specific reference could be to Ashurbanipal (669–633 BC) or, more likely, to Sennacherib (705–681 BC), who invaded Judah in 701 BC and of whom Isaiah speaks in similar language (see Isaiah 10:7). Belial is also used of Satan in 2 Corinthians 6:15. It is a way to describe evil, worthless, or wicked men (see Judges 19:22; 1 Samuel 2:12; 1 Kings 21:10, 13).

12. THUS SAYS THE LORD: Used as a common prophetic formula to introduce God's unequivocal message, it occurs only here in Nahum. Verse 12a is related in the third person, denoting the enemy, while in verse 12b the chosen people of God are spoken of in the second person. The safety of a walled city and massive numbers ("many") would not be a sufficient defense. "In this manner" harkens back to verses 7–10.

12B–13. I WILL AFFLICT YOU NO MORE: Judah was to be no longer oppressed by Assyria.

14. A COMMAND CONCERNING YOU: Three judgments on Assyria are pronounced. First, the king of Assyria, representing the nation, would become destitute of descendants. Second, the gods by which they received their authority would be destroyed. Third, the king would be put to death. This occurred in the fall of Nineveh in 612 BC.

15. MOUNTAINS . . . FEET: This verse echoes Isaiah 52:7, where it refers to those who announced the deliverance from Babylon. The theme of good tidings and peace reverberates throughout the message of the New Testament (see Luke 2:10; compare Isaiah 61:1 with Luke 4:16–21; Romans 10:15; Ephesians 2:14–18).

APPOINTED FEASTS: During a siege, people were prevented from going up to Jerusalem to celebrate her annual feasts (see Numbers 28–29). With the destruction of Assyria, Judah was called upon to celebrate her feasts and to pay the vows made while under siege (see Psalm 116:14, 17–18).

DESTRUCTION OF NINEVEH DETAILED: Nineveh's fall in 612 BC at the hands of Nebuchadnezzar of Babylon, though still future in Nahum's day, is described here vividly in present-tense terms.

2:1. SCATTERS: Assyria had made a practice of dispersing captives to many nations. Now she would receive similar judgment.

MAN . . . WATCH . . . STRENGTHEN: The prophet, with irony and satire, ordered the Assyrians to prepare for the coming invasion from Babylon.

2. EXCELLENCE OF JACOB . . . ISRAEL: This is not a reference to the southern and northern tribes—as the northern tribes had been overrun by Assyria almost a century earlier—but rather are titles of honor for Judah, remembering the day when Jacob received God's blessing at Peniel (see Genesis 32:27–28) and had his name changed to Israel. Together, they signify the nation's restoration to the promised position.

EMPTIERS HAVE EMPTIED THEM: Assyria had repeatedly "emptied" the land, destroying its fruitful vineyards and economic lifeblood.

3. SHIELDS . . . MADE RED: Shields were either overlaid with copper, whose reflections of sunshine would make the army appear larger and strike terror in the enemy, or they were covered with hide that was dyed red, so as to extinguish fiery arrows and to minimize the sight of blood. "Scarlet" clothing would have similar benefits.

SPEARS ARE BRANDISHED: Warriors, denoting their eagerness and readiness for battle, would wave their weapons.

4. THE CHARIOTS RAGE IN THE STREETS: Confusion reigned in Nineveh, where battle preparations were hurriedly made.

5. THEY MAKE HASTE TO HER WALLS: This may continue the thought of verse 4, depicting Nineveh's royalty and military leaders dashing to one of her many defense towers that, according to the Greek historian Diodorus Siculus, numbered 1,500 and reached a height of 200 feet. It is also possible that the latter part of the verse is a description of the attackers preparing to erect a "mantelet," a small fortress-type box in which soldiers rode for protection as they advanced to the wall.

6. GATES OF THE RIVERS: Nineveh, lying at the confluence of three rivers (the Tigris and two smaller rivers), constructed dams to minimize the damage of seasonal flooding to her walls. The latter part of verse 6 suggests that these dam gates were opened, causing the walls to be dissolved and the palace to be taken.

7. SHE SHALL BE LED AWAY CAPTIVE: The goddess of Nineveh, probably Ishtar, was taken away by her attackers to demonstrate the superiority of their gods (see 1 Samuel 4:1–11). The temple prostitutes ("maidservants") mourned the fate of their goddess.

8. POOL OF WATER: Although Nineveh was like an oasis in the desert that attracted many people, they fled from the devastation.

9. SPOIL: Spoils abounded in Nineveh, but it was her turn to be plundered.

10. HEART MELTS: The great city of Nineveh, lying in ruin, evoked fear and terror in those who observed it (see Daniel 5:6).

11–13. WHERE IS THE DWELLING OF THE LIONS: Archeologists have found a carving from a palace showing an Assyrian king on a lion hunt. Nahum rhetorically asked where Nineveh had gone. No longer describing Nineveh's fall, he taunted her, ridiculing her fall from power and glory. Like a pride of lions, with plenty to eat and in fear of no enemy, Nineveh ruthlessly "tore in pieces" (verse 12) her prey. She herself would now become prey for another nation, under the sovereign direction of God. "I am against you" (verse 13) should be the most feared words a nation could receive from God.

13. BURN YOUR CHARIOTS: Nineveh, known for burning captured cities, would receive the same fate.

YOUR MESSENGERS: The voice of the messengers who carried the edicts of the mighty king of Assyria to the captured nations would become mute.

> *DESTRUCTION OF NINEVEH DEMANDED: The prophet Nahum, asserting that the destruction of Nineveh was justly deserved, makes three charges against her (verses 1, 4, 8–10), followed by the consequences (verses 2–3, 5–7, 11–19).*

3:1. BLOODY CITY: The first accusation is a charge well documented in history. Assyria proved to be an unusually cruel, bloodthirsty nation.

LIES: Assyria employed falsehood and treachery to subdue her enemies (see 2 Kings 18:28–32).

ROBBERY: See Nahum 2:11–12. Preying upon her victims, she filled her cities with the goods of other nations.

2–3. STUMBLE OVER THE CORPSES: These verses reach back to the scene portrayed in Nahum 2:3–5. Assyria was so overrun that she was filled with corpses, causing the defenders to stumble over them.

4. MULTITUDE OF HARLOTRIES: The second charge against Nineveh was spiritual and moral harlotry. The nation was likened to a beautiful prostitute who seduced the nations with her illicit enticements.

5–6. SHOW THE NATIONS YOUR NAKEDNESS: Nineveh would be publicly exposed, resulting in shame and humiliation.

7. NINEVEH IS LAID WASTE: Instead of mourning, there would be rejoicing at her fall. None would be found to comfort her; she would bear her misery alone.

8–10. ARE YOU BETTER THAN NO AMON: Nahum sets forth the third and final charge against Nineveh: they had not learned from No Amon. Also known as Thebes, No Amon was the great capital of southern Egypt, located 400 miles south of Cairo. One of the most magnificent ancient civilizations of the world, it was renowned for its one hundred gates, a temple measuring 330 feet long and 170 feet wide, and its network of canals. It fell to Ashurbanipal of Assyria in 663 BC. Like No Amon by the Nile, Nineveh was situated by the Tigris River, enjoying the security of conquered nations around her. However, her end would be like that of No Amon.

9. ETHIOPIA . . . EGYPT . . . PUT . . . LUBIM: No Amon was well protected on all sides, nestled between lower Egypt on the north and Ethiopia on the south. The location of Put is best identified in the general vicinity of North Africa. Josephus, the first-century Jewish historian, said that Put, the third son of Ham (see Genesis 10:6), was the founder of Libya. Lubim has been identified with the area of modern Libya as well.

11. DRUNK: As predicted (see Nahum 1:10), Nineveh would be made to drink of God's wrath, making her drunk and defenseless to His judgment.

12–13. FIG TREES . . . WOMEN: Nahum employs a series of metaphors to emphasize that Nineveh's strong defenses would be easily overrun. Their walls would be like ripe fruit that falls at the slightest shaking and their battle forces like weak women.

14–15. FORTIFY YOUR STRONGHOLDS: The prophet taunts the people with sarcasm, urging them to prepare for battle, to fortify the city's defenses, only to be destroyed. As the locust leaves nothing, stripping all the foliage, so there would be nothing left of Nineveh (see Amos 7:1).

16. MULTIPLIED YOUR MERCHANTS: Nineveh had multiplied her merchants, bringing immense wealth, which only provided more to destroy.

17. LOCUSTS: Not only was Nineveh's commercial strength gone (see verse 16), but her governing resources disappeared as well. After camping for the night

within the massive walls of this great citadel, the locusts, depicting Assyria's leadership, flew away with the first rays of warm sunshine in search of food.

18. SLUMBER . . . REST: The Assyrian leaders and army, described in terms of exhaustion and sleep, were dead and the people were scattered. There were none left to help against the invasion of the Babylonians, to whom they fell in 612 BC.

19. NO HEALING: The destiny of Nineveh was certain. She had received the death blow—she would not recover—and all who heard of it would rejoice. Assyria had devastated the nations with her atrocities and cruelties; consequently, the news of her downfall brought happiness and mirth among the nations.

UNLEASHING THE TEXT

1) What does Nahum mean when he writes that "God is jealous" (1:2)? How had God shown that he was "slow to anger" (verse 3) toward Nineveh's transgressions in the past?

_____

_____

_____

_____

_____

_____

_____

2) Much of Nahum's prophecy deals with warfare and destruction, including violent imagery. How should we understand the presence of such violence in the pages of Scripture?

_____

_____

_____

_____

_____

_____

3) What are some possible reasons why God took special interest to declare His judgment and wrath against the city of Nineveh and its people?

_____

_____

_____

_____

_____

_____

_____

_____

4) How would you describe the overall theme of Nahum's prophetic book?

_____

_____

_____

_____

_____

_____

_____

EXPLORING THE MEANING

God Is True to His Word. The book of Nahum is a powerful illustration of God's sovereignty. Jonah had prophesied judgment against Nineveh about a hundred years before Nahum, stating, "Forty days, and Nineveh shall be overthrown" (Jonah 3:4). His prophecy sparked national repentance and God relented in carrying out His judgment (see verses 6–10). Sadly, that repentance did not last, and the people again gave themselves over to corruption, injustice, and idolatry. As a result, God spoke through Nahum to reaffirm His judgment against Nineveh— and that judgment ultimately *did* come to pass. This is an important lesson for us to remember. The Lord God is "gracious and merciful" (2 Chronicles 30:9), but He is also serious about the consequences of not turning away from sin. We would do well to take Him at His word.

The Word of God Is Truth. One of the most powerful elements of Nahum's prophecy is the accuracy with which it foretold the eventual destruction of Nineveh. Remember that Nahum delivered this prophecy decades before the city was destroyed. Even so, he was able to comment on the different stages and horrors of the sack of Nineveh as if he had personally witnessed the events. For instance, Nahum said Nineveh would end "with an overflowing flood" (1:8), and this happened when the Tigris River overflowed, destroying enough of the city walls to allow the Babylonian army to invade. Nahum also prophesied the city would "be hidden" (3:11), and this proved true because the city was not rediscovered after its destruction until AD 1842. Nahum's accuracy was bad news for Nineveh but good news for followers of Christ, for it reveals that *all* God's words are true. We can trust the accuracy and truth of the Bible.

Nothing Is Impossible for God. Assyria had been a tyrant on the world stage for centuries, known especially for her brutal treatment of captives and prisoners, both military and civilian. When Nahum emerged on the scene (c. 695–642 BC), Assyria was at the height of her power. Regardless, Nahum prophesied that God's people would soon no longer have to deal with this powerful empire: "Though I have afflicted you, I will afflict you no more; for now I will break off his yoke from you, and burst your bonds apart" (1:12–13). This was accomplished when the Babylonians brought down Nineveh in 612 BC, proving that no feat is too difficult for God. As Jesus said, "With men this is impossible, but with God all things are possible" (Matthew 19:26).

REFLECTING ON THE TEXT

5) The Bible reveals that God is always true to His word—that what He promises will happen will, in fact, occur. What are some examples of God's faithfulness in the Bible, church history, and your life?

_____

_____

_____

_____

_____

_____

_____

_____

6) The Bible contains many prophecies written long before the historical events they predicted. How should the truth of biblical prophecy affect believers?

_____

_____

_____

_____

_____

_____

_____

_____

7) Jesus said, "All things are possible to him who believes" (Mark 9:23). When have you witnessed this truth play out in your life?

_____

_____

_____

_____

_____

_____

_____

_____

8) God has declared, "Vengeance is Mine" (Deuteronomy 32:35). Why is it good for God to be wrathful? How is God's wrath different from man's wrath? How should believers respond to God's wrath? What about unbelievers?

_____

_____

_____

_____

_____

_____

_____

_____

PERSONAL RESPONSE

9) What are some specific promises and prophecies from God's Word that have served to impact your everyday life?

_____

_____

_____

_____

_____

_____

_____

10) What are some specific lessons that you have learned from the mistakes of your past? How will those lessons influence your future?

_____

_____

_____

_____

_____

_____

_____

7

A PROPHET'S PERPLEXITIES
Habakkuk 1:1–2:4

DRAWING NEAR

Make a list of people (living or dead) whom you would most like to engage in a conversation. What specifically would you talk about with each person?

_____

_____

_____

_____

_____

_____

_____

_____

_____

_____

_____

THE CONTEXT

As we explored in the previous lesson, the Assyrian Empire was overrun and conquered by a coalition of nations in 612 BC. This coalition was led by Nabopolassar, the founder and first king of the Neo-Babylonian Empire, who was later succeeded by his son Nebuchadnezzar. Thus, the Assyrian Empire was largely replaced on the world stage by the Babylonian Empire—a replacement that had major consequences for God's chosen people in Judah and Jerusalem.

Habakkuk ministered as a prophet during the fall of Assyria and the rise of Babylon. He was thus familiar with those nations and their influence on the region. For that reason, Habakkuk was greatly shocked when he learned that God intended to use the Babylonians as instruments of judgment against Judah and Jerusalem. The prophet understood the problem of sin and idolatry in Judah, but he was greatly perplexed by God's solution to that problem.

Structurally, the book of Habakkuk can be divided into three sections. In the first section, Habakkuk raises a poignant question and God responds (1:2–11). In the second section, Habakkuk raises another poignant question, and God responds a second time (1:12–2:20). In the third section, Habakkuk offers a prayer (or psalm) as an act of worship to the Lord (3:1–19).

KEYS TO THE TEXT
Read Habakkuk 1:1–2:4, noting the key words and phrases indicated below.

> THE PROPHET'S FIRST COMPLAINT: *In Habakkuk's first complaint,*
> *he perceives that God appears indifferent to Judah's sin. He questions*
> *God's wisdom, expressing bewilderment at His seeming inactivity*
> *in the face of blatant violations of His law.*

1:1. SAW: God's message to Habakkuk took the form of a vision.

2. HOW LONG SHALL I CRY: This phrase, reflecting the prophet's impatience, is frequently used by the psalmist to express similar thoughts of perplexity (see Psalms 13:1–2; 62:3; see also Jeremiah 14:9; Matthew 27:46). Habakkuk was jealous for God's righteousness and knew that a breach of the covenant required judgment (see Deuteronomy 28). The Jews had sinned by violence and injustice and should have been punished by the same.

2–3. VIOLENCE ... INIQUITY ... TROUBLE ... PLUNDERING: Habakkuk defines Judah's society using four terms that denote malicious wickedness by which one morally and ethically oppresses his neighbor, resulting in contention and strife.

2. AND YOU WILL NOT SAVE: The prophet wanted a cleansing, purging, chastening, and revival among the people that would return them to righteousness.

4. LAW IS POWERLESS: Literally the "law is chilled, numbed" (see Genesis 45:26; Psalm 77:2). It had no respect and was given no authority. As hands rendered useless by the cold, the effectiveness of the law was paralyzed by the corruption of Judah's leaders (see Ecclesiastes 8:11).

GOD'S FIRST RESPONSE: In response to Habakkuk's perplexity and pleading, God breaks His silence, informing him that He was not indifferent to Judah's sin. But rather than revival, He was sending "terrible and dreadful" judgment (verse 7).

5. LOOK . . . WATCH . . . BE UTTERLY ASTOUNDED: The series of commands is plural, indicating that the wider community of Judah and Jerusalem was to take note of this imminent invasion. Paul later quoted this text in Acts 13:41.

6–8. I AM RAISING UP THE CHALDEANS: The Chaldeans (Babylonians) would come at the behest of the divine commander. He was the Sovereign who would bring this people of ruthless character and conduct to invade Judah. The Babylonians are described as self-assured, self-sufficient, self-deified, and deadly (see Jeremiah 51:20).

8. EVENING WOLVES: These were wolves who had suffered hunger all day long and were forced to prowl into the night for food. Like wolves, Babylon's army displayed extraordinary stamina and an undaunted eagerness to attack for the purpose of devouring the spoils of victory.

10. THEY SCOFF AT KINGS: Whether it be royal authority or physical obstacles, the Babylonian army marched forward with nothing but scorn for those in their path.

HEAP UP EARTHEN MOUNDS: Rubble and dirt were piled up against the fortress or city wall as a ramp to gain entry.

11. TO HIS GOD: Although the Babylonians were God's instruments of judgment, their self-sufficiency and self-adulation planted the seeds for their own destruction (described in Habakkuk 2:2–20), as they stood guilty of idolatry and blasphemy before the sovereign Lord.

THE PROPHET'S SECOND COMPLAINT: Habakkuk, reacting to this perplexing revelation from God, first declares his confidence in the Lord and then unveils his second complaint—namely, how could the Lord use a wicked nation (the Babylonians) to judge a nation (Judah) who was more righteous than they were?

12. O LORD MY GOD . . . HOLY ONE: Although Habakkuk could not fully comprehend the sovereign workings of his righteous God, he nevertheless expressed his complete faith and trust in Him. As he rehearsed the unchangeable

character of God as eternal, sovereign, and holy, he became assured that Judah would not be completely destroyed (see Jeremiah 31:35–40; 33:23–26). Under the faithful hand of God, he realized that the Babylonians were coming to correct, not annihilate.

O ROCK: A title for God that expresses His immovable and unshakable character (see Psalms 18:2, 31, 46; 31:2–3; 62:2, 6–7; 78:16, 20, 35).

13. PURER EYES: In spite of the prophet's expressions of faith, he found himself in even further perplexity. The essence of Habakkuk's next quandary is expressed in this verse: If God is too pure to behold evil, then how can He use the wicked to devour a person more righteous than they? Would not God's use of the Babylonians result in even greater damage to His righteous character?

14–17. LIKE FISH OF THE SEA: Lest God had forgotten just how wicked the Babylonians were, Habakkuk drew attention to their evil character and behavior. Life was cheap to the Babylonians. In the face of their ruthless tactics of war, other societies were "like fish of the sea, like creeping things that have no ruler over them" (verse 14). In light of their reputation, how could God have unleashed this ruthless force upon another helpless people?

16. SACRIFICE ... BURN INCENSE TO THEIR DRAGNET: If that were not enough, the prophet added that the Babylonians attributed their gain to their own military might rather than to the true God.

17. EMPTY THEIR NET: How long would the aggressor (the Babylonians) be permitted to pursue injustice and engage in such wickedness? Would God tolerate it indefinitely?

2:1. STAND MY WATCH: The prophet ends his complaint by expressing his determination to wait for an answer. Comparing himself to a watchman (see Ezekiel 3:17ff.; 33:7–11), standing as a sentinel upon the city walls, Habakkuk prepared to wait for God and ponder His reply.

> GOD'S SECOND RESPONSE: *In response to Habakkuk's second complaint, the Lord announces that He will judge the Babylonians as well for their wickedness.*

2–3. WRITE THE VISION: God's reply included instructions for Habakkuk to record the vision to preserve it for posterity, so that all who read it would know of the certainty of its fulfillment (see similar language in Daniel 12:4, 9). The prophecy had lasting relevance and, thus, had to be preserved. Although a period of time would occur before its fulfillment, all were to know that it would occur at God's "appointed time" (see Isaiah 13; Jeremiah 50, 51). Babylon would fall to the Medo-Persian kingdom of Cyrus c. 539 BC (see Daniel 5).

2. THAT HE MAY RUN WHO READS IT: This could refer to (1) clarity of form, so that even the one who runs by it may easily absorb its meaning; or (2) clarity of content, so that the courier could easily transmit the message to others.

4. BEHOLD THE PROUD: God's reply also included this description of the character of the wicked in comparison to the righteous. While the context makes "the proud" an obvious reference to the Babylonians, the passage introduces the marks that distinguish all wicked people from all righteous, regardless of ethnic origin. Two opposing characteristics are here contrasted: (1) the proud trusts in himself, while (2) the just lives by his faith.

THE JUST SHALL LIVE BY HIS FAITH: In contrast to the proud, the just will be truly preserved through his faithfulness to God. This is the core of God's message to/through Habakkuk. Both the aspect of justification by faith, as noted by Paul's usage in Romans 1:17 and Galatians 3:11, as well as the aspect of sanctification by faith, as employed by the writer of Hebrews (10:38), reflect the essence of Habakkuk; no conflict exists between the two. The emphasis in both Habakkuk and the New Testament references goes beyond the act of faith to include the continuity of faith. Faith is not a one-time act but a way of life. The true believer, declared righteous by God, will persevere in faith as the pattern of life (see Colossians 1:22–23; Hebrews 3:12–14).

UNLEASHING THE TEXT

1) Summarize Habakkuk's first question to the Lord in 1:1–4. What problem was he addressing with God in this passage?

_____

_____

_____

_____

2) What is interesting about God's answer in 1:5–11? Why?

_____

_____

_____

_____

3) Summarize Habakkuk's second question to God in 1:12–17. What problem was he addressing with God in this passage?

_____

_____

_____

_____

_____

4) What is meant by God's statement that "the just shall live by his faith" (2:4)?

_____

_____

_____

_____

EXPLORING THE MEANING

God Acts in His Own Timing. Like most of the Old Testament prophets, Habakkuk ministered among a people who were far from God. The residents of Judah and Jerusalem had given themselves over to idolatry. Again and again, they refused God's call to repent and return to Him. From Habakkuk's point of view, the people did evil without fearing punishment of any kind, and so he cried out, "Oh LORD, how long shall I cry, and You will not hear?" (1:2). The prophet wanted to know *when God would do something about the problem*. Of course, with the benefit of hindsight, we know that God had already raised up judgment against Judah through the armies of Babylon. Yet we, too, often question God's timing. We wonder whether He sees the same problems we see—and we long for Him to fix those problems today rather than tomorrow. As with Habakkuk, the answer to our frustrations is to fully trust God to work in His own way and in His own time rather than fretting about circumstances we cannot control.

God Acts in His Own Ways. We do not always like the way that God chooses to respond to our requests. We prefer Him to do things the way that *we* want them done. But as Habakkuk learned, God acts according to His own will. The prophet wanted a cleansing, purging, chastening, and revival among the people that would return them to righteousness. Instead, God said that He was going to use the Babylonians to render judgment against them. This raised another question for Habakkuk: "Why do You . . . hold Your tongue when the wicked devours a person more righteous than he?" (1:13). He had a difficult time imagining how God could use such an ungodly people to lay hold of His holy city. Yet in the end, Habakkuk did not allow his questions *of* God to push him away *from* God. He affirmed that he would trust God regardless of his questions and confusion: "I will stand my watch and set myself on the rampart, and watch to see what He will say to me, and what I will answer when I am corrected" (2:1).

God Loves a Humble Heart. As we have seen, Habakkuk was deeply dismayed by the news that Babylon would serve as the instrument of justice against God's people in Judah. He asked the Lord, "Shall they therefore . . . continue to slay nations without pity?" (1:17). God answered that the Babylonians would also receive judgment for their wickedness—including their pride. The Lord added, "Behold the proud, his soul is not upright in him; but the just shall live by his faith" (2:4). This verse sets up an important dichotomy for us. We can live according to our own strength and resources, which leads to pride. Or we can submit to God's strength and resources, which requires faith. The Bible reveals where the first path leads: "Pride goes before destruction, and a haughty spirit before a fall" (Proverbs 16:18). But those who submit to the Lord in faith receive the promise that God "gives grace to the humble" (James 4:6).

REFLECTING ON THE TEXT

5) Followers of Jesus are to "wait on the LORD" (Isaiah 40:31). What does that look like in your life? What does it mean for you to wait for God's timing?

_____

_____

_____

_____

6) How do you typically respond when you, like Habakkuk, are frustrated by God's timing and seeming lack of action? How should you respond?

_____

_____

_____

_____

7) We all understand intellectually that God's ways are "higher than [our] ways" (Isaiah 55:9)—yet we still kick against His plans. What does it mean to truly submit to God's will?

_____

_____

_____

_____

_____

_____

8) Why is pride so sinful in God's eyes? Why is it important to humble oneself?

_____

_____

_____

_____

_____

_____

PERSONAL RESPONSE

9) What is causing you to feel confused or frustrated about the injustice or corruption that you see in the world? How can you bring those feelings before God?

_____

_____

_____

_____

_____

10) Where do you have an opportunity this week to trust God without fully understanding what He is doing? What would it take for you to exercise this type of trust in Him?

_____

_____

_____

_____

_____

8

A Prophet's Prayer

Habukkuk 2:5–3:19

Drawing Near

What are some ways worship and singing have been helpful in your relationship with God?

_____

_____

_____

_____

_____

_____

_____

_____

_____

_____

_____

_____

_____

The Context

Habakkuk was not only willing to converse with God but also ask questions of Him. First, the prophet wanted to know why God had waited so long to bring judgment against the people of Judah who were indulging in open sin and spiritual rebellion. Habakkuk likely had in mind the curses that Moses prophesied would come upon the Israelites if they failed to obey the Lord and observe His commandments and statutes (see Deuteronomy 28:15–68).

When God replied that His judgment was already in motion through the rise of the Babylonians (also known as the Chaldeans) and their armies, Habakkuk then questioned why God would use such an ungodly nation as a tool against His chosen people. The prophet had assumed that God would *save* the residents of Judah and Jerusalem (see Habakkuk 1:2)—that He would astonish them into repentance rather than destroy them. He wanted a revival among God's people that would return them to righteousness.

As we will explore in this lesson, God's reponse to this second complaint from His prophet was that the Babylonians would also not escape His divine judgment. God even went so far as to proclaim five separate "woes" that would befall the different classes of evildoers in Babylonian society. Following this response, the prophet realized the time for questioning was concluded. Habakkuk instead adopted a posture of prayer and praise, ending his prophetic book by expressing his steadfast faith and trust in the Lord God.

KEYS TO THE TEXT

Read Habakkuk 2:5–3:19, noting the key words and phrases indicated below.

> FIVE WOES: *Continuing His response to Habakkuk's second complaint (1:12–2:1), the Lord pronounces five woes, in the form of a taunt song, upon the Babylonians in anticipation of their eventual judgment. Presented in five stanzas of three verses each, the five woes are directed at five different classes of evildoers.*

2:5. HE TRANSGRESSES: The diatribe of this verse serves as the basis for the denunciations that will be described in verses 6–20. The Babylonians were proud and greedy. Like hell and death (see Proverbs 1:12; 27:20; 30:15–16), they were never satisfied but always wanted more.

6–8. WOE TO HIM WHO INCREASES: "Woe" is an interjection often used in prophetic literature to introduce a judicial indictment or a sentence of judgment (see Isaiah 5:8, 11, 18, 20–22; Jeremiah 22:13; 23:1; Amos 5:18; 6:1). The first woe charged extortion; that is, the Babylonians' plundering of other nations under threat of great bodily harm for the purpose of making themselves rich. As a result, they were to become plunder for those nations who remained.

6. ALL THESE: A reference to all the nations that suffered at the hands of the Babylonians.

MANY PLEDGES: The Babylonians exacted heavy taxation on conquered nations. Such action often accompanied loans with excessive interest made to the poor (see Deuteronomy 24:10–13; 2 Kings 4:1–7; Nehemiah 5:1–13).

7. YOUR CREDITORS: The survivor nations, from whom taxation was extorted (see verse 8).

9–11. WOE TO HIM WHO COVETS: God's second charge, of premeditated exploitation borne out of covetousness, is a continuation of verses 6–8. The walls of the Babylonians' houses, built with stones and timbers taken from others, testified against them (verse 11).

9. SET HIS NEST ON HIGH: The Babylonians, wanting to protect themselves from any recriminations their enemies might seek to shower upon them, had sought to make their cities impregnable and inaccessible to the enemy (see Isaiah 14:13–14).

10. YOU GIVE SHAMEFUL COUNSEL: The Babylonian leaders, by counseling to kill, had shamed themselves and harmed their souls.

12–14. WOE TO HIM WHO BUILDS . . . WITH BLOODSHED: God's third woe accused them of being ruthless despots, building luxurious palaces by means of bloodshed and forced labor. Like a fire that burns everything given to it, their labors would all be futile, having no lasting value (verse 13; see Micah 3:10).

14. FILLED: In contrast to the self-exaltation of the Babylonians, whose efforts would come to naught, God promised that the whole earth would recognize His glory at the establishment of His millennial kingdom (see Numbers 14:21; Psalm 72:19; Isaiah 6:3; 11:9).

15–17. WOE TO HIM WHO GIVES DRINK: God's fourth charge against the Babylonians was debauchery, wherein they had forced others to become intoxicated and poisoned, making them behave shamefully and become easy prey. As a result, they too would be forced to drink the cup of God's wrath and be exposed to public shame (see Jeremiah 49:12).

16. UNCIRCUMCISED: This word refers to "foreskin," expressing in Hebrew thought the greatest contempt—the sign of being an alien from God. The purpose of circumcision (see Genesis 17:10–14) was to cut away flesh that could hold disease in its folds and thus pass the disease on to wives. It was important for the preservation of God's people physically. But it was also a symbol of the need for the heart to be cleansed from sin's deadly disease.

CUP OF THE LORD'S RIGHT HAND: A metaphor referring to divine retribution, served up by His powerful right hand (see Psalm 21:8). What the Babylonians had done to others would also be done to them (see Habakkuk 2:7–8).

SHAME WILL BE ON YOUR GLORY: Carrying out the metaphor of drunkenness, this is a reference to the humiliation of "shameful spewing." The very thing in which the Babylonians gloried would become the object of their shame. While the Lord's glory would be "as the waters cover the sea" (verse 14), their glory would be covered with shame.

17. VIOLENCE: This reference may be to the ruthless exploitation of trees and animals—providing building materials, firewood, and food—that often accompanied military campaigns. Lebanon's beautiful cedars were plundered for selfish purposes (see Isaiah 14:7–8; 37:24).

MEN'S BLOOD: This refers to the slaughter of men, possibly Israel and her inhabitants, whom Nebuchadnezzar conquered (see 2 Kings 14:9; Jeremiah 22:6, 23; Ezekiel 17:3).

18–20. WOE TO HIM WHO SAYS TO WOOD, "AWAKE!": God's fifth accusation against the Babylonians is idolatry, exposing the folly of following other gods (see Isaiah 41:24; 44:9). The destruction of the Babylonians would demonstrate the superiority of the Lord over all gods.

19. "AWAKE!" . . . "ARISE!": Compare the sarcasm with that of Elijah's words to the prophets of Baal on Mount Carmel in 1 Kings 18:27 (see also Jeremiah 2:27).

20. HOLY TEMPLE: A reference to heaven, from where the Lord rules (see Psalm 11:4) and answers the prayers of those who seek Him (see 1 Kings 8:28–30; Psalm 73:17).

KEEP SILENCE: In contrast to the silence of the idols (verse 19), the living, Sovereign Ruler of the universe calls all the earth to be silent before Him. None can assert his independence from Him; all the earth must worship in humble submission (see Psalm 46:10; Isaiah 52:15).

> THE PROPHET'S PRAYER: *The argumentative tone of Habakkuk's previous chapters, in which he cries out for divine mercy, is transformed into a plea for God's mercy.*

3:1. HABAKKUK THE PROPHET: This reference to the prophet marks a transition. Habakkuk will now plead for God's mercy (verse 2), review God's power (verses 3–15), and offer a chorus of praise for God's sustaining grace and sufficiency (verses 16–19). But while the tone changes, a strong, thematic connection remains. Having been informed of God's plan of judgment, Habakkuk returns to the matter of Judah's judgment, pleading for mercy.

SHIGIONOTH: The precise meaning is unknown (its singular form occurs in the heading to Psalm 7). In light of the musical notation at the end of Habakkuk 3, it is thought that this has a musical-liturgical significance and that this chapter was sung.

2. YOUR SPEECH: A reference back to Habakkuk 1:5–11 and 2:2–20, where the Lord informed the prophet of His plans for judging Judah and the Babylonians.

REVIVE YOUR WORK: Knowledge of the severity of God's judgment struck Habakkuk with fear. As though God's power had not been used in a long time, the prophet asked the Lord to "revive" (literally "to quicken"), to repeat His mighty saving works on behalf of His people, Israel.

MIDST OF THE YEARS: In the midst of God's punishment of Judah at the hand of the Babylonians, the prophet begged that God would remember mercy.

3–15. GOD CAME: Employing figures from God's past intervention on Israel's behalf, taken from the deliverance of His people from Egypt and the conquest of Canaan, Habakkuk paints a picture of their future redemption. The Exodus from Egypt is often used as an analogy of the future redemption of Israel at the beginning of the Millennium (see Isaiah 11:16).

3. TEMAN: Teman, named after a grandson of Esau, was an Edomite city (see Amos 1:12; Obadiah 1:9).

MOUNT PARAN: Mount Paran was located in the Sinai peninsula. Both allude to the theater in which God displayed great power when He brought Israel into the land of Canaan (see Deuteronomy 33:2; Judges 5:4).

3–4. HIS GLORY: The Shekinah glory, which protected and led Israel from Egypt through the wilderness (see Exodus 40:34–38), was the physical manifestation of His presence. Like the sun, He spread His radiance throughout the heavens and the earth.

5. PESTILENCE . . . FEVER: Recalling the judgment attending Israel's disobedience to the covenant given at Sinai (see Exodus 5:3; Numbers 14:12; Deuteronomy 28:21–22; 32:24), Habakkuk accentuates the sovereign agency of God's judgments. Both were a part of the divine entourage.

6–7. THE EVERLASTING MOUNTAINS WERE SCATTERED: The entire universe responds in fear at the approach of Almighty God (see Exodus 15:14). As at the Creation (Isaiah 40:12), the earth and its inhabitants are at His disposal.

7. CUSHAN ... MIDIAN: Probably referring to one people living in the Sinai peninsula region. Moses' wife was identified as being both Midianite and Cushite (see Exodus 2:16–22; 18:1–5; Numbers 12:1).

8–15. O LORD, WERE YOU DISPLEASED: With rhetorical vividness, Habakkuk addresses the Lord directly, rehearsing His judicial actions against anything that opposes His will.

YOUR HORSES ... YOUR CHARIOTS: Symbolic descriptions of God defeating the enemy (see Habakkuk 3:11, 15).

9. OATHS WERE SWORN OVER YOUR ARROWS: The Lord's arrows were commissioned under divine oaths (see Jeremiah 47:6–7).

11. SUN AND MOON STOOD STILL: As prominent symbols of God's created order, the sun and moon are subservient to His beckoning. The imagery is reminiscent of Israel's victory over the Amorites at Gibeon (see Joshua 10:12–14).

12. TRAMPLED: Literally "threshed," the term is often used to depict military invasions and the execution of judgment (see Judges 8:7; 2 Kings 13:7; Isaiah 21:10; 25:10; Daniel 7:23; Amos 1:3).

13. SALVATION WITH YOUR ANOINTED: Both the parallelism with verse 13a ("salvation of Your people") and numerous contextual allusions to the Exodus make this a likely reference to Moses and the chosen people of Israel, who, as God's anointed, achieved victory over Pharaoh and the armies of Egypt (see Psalm 105:15). Ultimately, it foreshadows a subsequent, future deliverance in anticipation of the Messiah (see Psalm 132:10–12) promised in the Davidic covenant (see 2 Samuel 7:11–16).

STRUCK THE HEAD FROM THE HOUSE OF THE WICKED: A possible reference to either the pharaoh of the Exodus, whose firstborn was slain, or the king of the Babylonians, whose house was built by unjust gain (see Habakkuk 2:9–11).

14. THEY CAME OUT ... TO SCATTER: A possible reference to the pursuit of fleeing Israel at the Red Sea by Pharaoh's army (see Exodus 14:5–9). Like the poor, Israel appeared to be easy prey for the pursuing Egyptians.

15. YOU WALKED THROUGH THE SEA: Another reference to God's miraculous, protective intervention on behalf of Israel at the Red Sea. The historical event demonstrates His sovereign rulership of the universe and provides assurance to the troubled prophet that the Lord could be counted on to save His people once more.

16–19. REST IN THE DAY OF TROUBLE: Habakkuk ended his prophecy with renewed commitment and affirmation of faith, expressing unwavering confidence in God. The Lord had answered his prayer (verse 1); He would vindicate His righteousness and ultimately restore a truly repentant people (see 2:4). While the answer satisfied Habakkuk, the thought of a Babylonian invasion of his people also left him physically exhausted and overwhelmed (see Jeremiah 4:19). Nevertheless, the prophet could "rest in the day of trouble" because he knew the Lord would judge righteously.

17–18. I WILL REJOICE IN THE LORD: If everything that was normal and predictable collapsed, the prophet would still rejoice. Obedience to the covenant was a requisite element to the enjoyment of agricultural and pastoral prosperity (see Deuteronomy 28:1–14). Although disobedience would initiate the covenant curses (see Deuteronomy 28:31–34, 49–51), the prophet affirmed his commitment to the Lord; his longing and joyful desire was for God Himself.

19. THE LORD GOD IS MY STRENGTH: God's response to Habakkuk's perplexities not only promised divine wrath but also provided assurance of divine favor and hope. Security and hope were not based on temporal blessings but on the Lord Himself. This is the essence of Habukkuk 2:4: "the just shall live by his faith."

LIKE DEER'S FEET: As the sure-footed deer scaled the precipitous mountain heights without slipping, so Habakkuk's faith in the Lord enabled him to endure the hardships of the imminent invasion and all of his perplexing questions.

TO THE CHIEF MUSICIAN: This chapter possibly served as a psalm for temple worship (see verse 1).

UNLEASHING THE TEXT

1) God's denunciation of the Babylonians came to the prophet Habakkuk in five separate woes (see 2:5–20). Which of those "woes" is the most devastating? Why that particular woe?

_____

_____

_____

_____

_____

_____

_____

_____

_____

_____

2) Summarize God's overall charge against the Babylonians. What was His message concerning their present and their future?

_____

_____

_____

_____

_____

3) What are some of the key images from Habakkuk's prayer (or psalm) in 3:1–19? What do those images communicate?

_____

_____

_____

_____

_____

4) What emotions did Habakkuk express or imply throughout that prayer?

_____

_____

_____

_____

EXPLORING THE MEANING

Beware the Five Woes. God's response to Habakkuk's second complaint included five "woes" or indictments against five different classes of evildoers: (1) those who *extort* from others, (2) those who *covet* (are greedy), (3) those who are *violent* toward others, (4) those who engage in *debauchery*, and (5) those who practice *idolatry.* These actions and attitudes create poverty, violence, and societal ruin in our world today and wreak havoc in our personal lives. This is why God instructs us to reject these sinful practices and instead seek a deeper connection with Him: "But the LORD is in His holy temple. Let all the earth keep silence before Him" (2:20). God desires us to sit in silence before Him, waiting for His instructions to guide our lives.

Worship God for Who He Is. As limited human beings who worship a limitless God, we can fall into the error of defining our relationship with God by what He can do for us—worshiping Him not because of who He is but because of the blessings He provides. This leads to a transactional relationship, as if God were a divine vending machine. Early in Habakkuk, we find the prophet meditating on what he wants God to do; namely, punish the wicked in Judah. He then wants God to spare those same evildoers from the wrath of Babylon. But in Habakkuk 3, we find the prophet focusing more on God's attributes than His actions. Habakkuk praises God's nature and character, including both His mercy and strength. The psalm ends with a reflection on worshiping God even when circumstances are difficult: "Though the fig tree may not blossom, nor fruit be on the vines; though the labor of the olive may fail, and the fields yield no food; though the flock may be cut off from the fold, and there be no herd in the stalls—yet I will rejoice in the LORD, I will joy in the God of my salvation" (verses 17–18).

Bring Your Questions to God. Habakkuk was not afraid to approach the Lord with the deepest questions on his heart. His words are reminiscent of the psalmists, who wrote statements such as, "O God . . . will the enemy blaspheme Your name forever?" (74:10), and, "My God, My God, why have You forsaken Me?" (22:1). God responded to Habakkuk's questions not with scorn but with answers. He will do the same for us. In fact, God actually *invites* us to bring our questions to Him! As He told Jeremiah, "Call to Me, and I will answer you, and show you great and mighty things, which you do not know" (33:3). The author of Hebrews added that we can approach Him with confidence: "Let us therefore come boldly to the throne of grace, that we may obtain mercy" (4:16).

Reflecting on the Text

5) Look again at the five "woes" declared against Babylon in Habakkuk 2:5–19. What are some connections between those woes and our culture today?

_____

_____

_____

_____

_____

_____

6) How can you tell if your relationship with God is being defined more by what He can do for you than who He is? What are symptoms of that condition?

_____

_____

_____

_____

7) If you are basing your relationship with God on what He does for you—a transactional relationship—what is the solution to that problem?

_____

_____

_____

_____

8) While believers ought to bring their questions to God in prayer, should they expect Him to answer in the same way He responded to Habakkuk? How does God speak to believers today?

_____

_____

_____

_____

Personal Response

9) What steps will you take this week to learn more about God's character?

_____

_____

_____

_____

10) Where do you have an opportunity this week to demonstrate your trust in God?

_____

_____

_____

_____

9

AN ILLUSTRATION OF DEVASTATION
Joel 1:1–2:17

DRAWING NEAR
What are some ways that your life has been impacted by natural disasters?

THE CONTEXT

Prophets have been known throughout history as those who speak God's words to humanity. More specifically, prophets are typically associated with God's words of warning and judgment. We think of a prophet as someone standing in opposition to the people and leaders of his day, crying out "Repent!" or "The end is near!" Certainly, many of the prophets were charged with confronting the people because of their sin and providing warnings of future judgment.

There are many ways in which Joel operated as this kind of prophet. He ministered to the Israelites during a difficult season. The Jewish people were being harassed by enemy armies and had just endured a series of plague-like locust swarms that had devastated their crops—a horrible scenario for an agrarian society. God had charged Joel with using those circumstances as an opportunity to warn His people about judgment at the future "Day of the Lord."

Yet as we will explore in this lesson, God's intent in making this charge to His prophet was to turn His people's hearts back to Him in repentance. "'Now, therefore,' says the LORD, 'Turn to Me with all your heart'" (Joel 2:12). The Lord wanted His priests to cry out, "Spare Your people, O LORD" (verse 17). In this way, God would demonstrate His mercy to them.

KEYS TO THE TEXT

Read Joel 1:1–2:17, noting the key words and phrases indicated below.

> THE LAND LAID WASTE: *Joel describes the contemporary Day of the Lord. The land was suffering massive devastation caused by a locust plague and drought.*

1:1. THE WORD OF THE LORD: This introductory phrase is frequently employed by the prophets to indicate that the message was divinely commissioned (see Hosea 1:1; Micah 1:1; Zephaniah 1:1). Slightly varied forms are found in 1 Samuel 15:10; 2 Samuel 24:11; Jeremiah 1:2; Ezekiel 1:3; Jonah 1:1; Zechariah 1:1; Malachi 1:1.

LORD: A distinctively Israelitish designation for God; the name speaks of intimacy and a relationship bonded metaphorically through the covenant that is likened to marriage and, thus, carries special significance to Israel (see Exodus 3:14).

JOEL: His name means "the Lord is God."

PETHUEL: His name means "openheartedness of/toward God" and is the only occurrence of this name in the Bible.

2. HEAR ... GIVE EAR: The gravity of the situation demanded the undivided focus of their senses, emphasizing the need to make a conscious, purposeful decision in the matter. The terminology was commonly used in "lawsuit" passages (see Isaiah 1:2; Hosea 4:1), intimating that Israel was found guilty and that the present judgment was her "sentence." The details of the calamity that Joel will next outline (verses 2–12) will be followed by a summons to corporate penitence and reformation (verses 13–20).

ELDERS ... ALL YOU INHABITANTS: The term "elders" refers to the civil and religious leaders, who, in light of their position, were exhorted to lead by example the entire population (latter phrase) toward repentance. The historical severity of devastation should have warned the population that this was divine chastisement, not just a bad natural cycle of events.

3. TELL ... CHILDREN ... ANOTHER GENERATION: The pedagogical importance of reciting the Lord's mighty acts to subsequent generations is heavily underscored by this threefold injunction (see Exodus 10:1–6; Deuteronomy 4:9; 6:6–7; 11:19; 32:7; Psalms 78:5–7; 145:4–7; Proverbs 4:1ff.).

4. CHEWING ... SWARMING ... CRAWLING ... CONSUMING LOCUST: The four kinds of locusts refer to their different species or their stages of development (they are mentioned in different order in Joel 2:25). The total destruction caused by their voracious appetites demands repentance to avoid future, repeat occurrences (see Deuteronomy 28:38; Isaiah 33:4; Amos 7:1).

5–12. YOU DRUNKARDS ... PRIESTS ... FARMERS: Total destruction affected all social and economic levels. Affected were the drunkards who delighted in the abundance of the vine (verses 5–7), the priests who utilized the produce in the offerings (verses 8–10), and the farmers who planted, cultivated, and reaped the harvest (verses 11–12). As if building toward a crescendo, the prophet notes in the first stanza that the luxuries of life were withdrawn. In the second, the elements needed to worship were interrupted. In the third, the essentials for living were snatched away. To lose the enjoyment of wine was one thing; to no longer be able to worship God outwardly was another; but to have nothing to eat was the sentence of death!

5. AWAKE ... WEEP ... WAIL: The drunkards were to awaken to the realization that their wine would be no more. They were to weep bitterly and to wail. The severity of the devastation called for public, communal mourning.

NEW WINE: Occasionally translated "sweet wine," the term can denote either freshly squeezed grape juice or newly fermented wine (see Isaiah 49:26).

6–7. MY LAND . . . VINE . . . FIG TREE: The possessive pronoun refers to the Lord. He is the owner of the land (see Leviticus 25:23; Numbers 36:2; Ezekiel 38:16), the vine, and the fig tree (see Hosea 2:9). Instead of symbols for prosperity and peace (see 1 Kings 4:25; Micah 4:4; Zechariah 3:10), the vine and fig tree had become visual reminders of divine judgment.

6. A NATION: A literal invasion of locusts pictured the kind of destruction and judgment inflicted by human armies.

HIS TEETH ARE THE TEETH OF A LION: Joel describes these hostile, countless locusts as possessing the "fangs of a fierce lion," so able were they to devour anything in their path. Lions are occasionally used as symbolic of violence (see Genesis 49:9; Numbers 23:24) and of the violent, awesome nature of God's judgment (see Isaiah 30:6; Hosea 13:8).

8–9. LAMENT LIKE A VIRGIN: The Old Testament speaks of God as the husband of Israel, His wife (see Isaiah 54:5–8; Jeremiah 31:32). As with the drunkards, the religious leaders were to lament as a young maiden would on the death of her youthful husband, wherein she exchanged the silky fabric of a wedding dress and the joy of a wedding feast for sackcloth and the cry of a funeral dirge. The term "virgin" lacks the notion of virginity in many cases (for example, Esther 2:17; Ezekiel 23:3); and when coupled together with the term "husband," points to a young maiden widowed shortly after marriage.

SACKCLOTH: Fabric generally made of goat's hair, usually black or dark in color (see Revelation 6:12), and usually placed on the bare body around the hips (see Genesis 37:34; 1 Kings 21:27), leaving the chest free for "beating" (see Isaiah 32:11–12), was used in the ancient world to depict sorrow and penitence (see Nehemiah 9:1; Isaiah 37:1; Matthew 11:21). Because the prophets' message usually dealt with a call to repentance, it became the principal garment worn by prophets (see Matthew 3:4; Revelation 11:3).

9. GRAIN OFFERING . . . DRINK OFFERING HAVE BEEN CUT OFF: The covenantal offerings and libations could not be carried out; therefore, Israel, the wife of the Lord, was to repent, lest her relationship with the Lord became like that of the young widowed maiden. To cut off these offerings, sacrificed each morning and evening (see Exodus 29:38–42; Leviticus 23:13), was to cut off the people from the covenant. The gravity of the situation was deepened by the fact that it threatened the livelihood of the priests, who were given a portion of most sacrifices.

11. BE ASHAMED, YOU FARMERS: The primary emphasis of the Hebrew term connotes a public disgrace, a physical state to which the guilty party has been forcibly brought.

12. ALL THE TREES OF THE FIELD ARE WITHERED: The picture was bleak, for even the deep roots of the trees could not withstand the torturous treatment administered by the locusts, especially when accompanied by an extended drought (see verse 20).

JOY HAS WITHERED: Human joy and delight had departed from all segments of society; none had escaped the grasp of the locusts. The joy that normally accompanied the time of harvest had been replaced by despair.

A CALL TO REPENT: Joel calls on the priests to take action, first by example and then by proclamation. As the leaders, it was their duty to proclaim a public fast so the entire nation could repent and petition the Lord to forgive and restore. He admonishes them to "consecrate" a fast, denoting its urgent, sacred character.

14. CALL A SACRED ASSEMBLY: Directives for calling an assembly, generally for festive purposes (see 2 Chronicles 7:9; Nehemiah 8:18), are given in Numbers 10:3. Parallel in thought to "consecrate a fast," no work was permitted on such days (see Leviticus 23:36; Numbers 29:35; Deuteronomy 16:8).

15. THE DAY OF THE LORD IS AT HAND: This is the first occurrence of this major theme in Joel (see 2:1, 11, 31; 3:14). Later in the book (2:18ff.; 3:1, 18–21), the Day of the Lord—the occasion when God pours out His wrath on man—results in blessing and exoneration for God's people and judgment toward Gentiles (see Isaiah 13:6; Ezekiel 30:3), but here Joel directed the warning toward his own people. The Day of the Lord was at hand; unless sinners repented, dire consequences awaited them.

DESTRUCTION FROM THE ALMIGHTY: The Hebrew term "destruction" forms a powerful play on words with the "Almighty." The notion of invincible strength is foremost; destruction at the hand of the omnipotent God was coming. Their calamity was not from some freak turn of nature but rather from the purposeful punishment of their Creator God.

17–18. SEED SHRIVELS . . . ANIMALS GROAN: From the spiritual realm to the physical realm, all was in shambles. Though innocent, in judgment even the animals suffered (see Romans 8:18–22) the loss of food.

19. TO YOU I CRY OUT: As the first one to call the nation to repentance, the prophet had to be the first to heed the warning. He had to lead by example and motivate the people to respond. In the midst of proclaiming judgment, God's prophets often led in intercessory prayer for mercy and forgiveness (see Exodus 32:11–14; Jeremiah 42:1–4; Daniel 9:1–19; Amos 7:1–6).

FIRE: Because the locust devastation was so severe and thorough, it was compared to a destroyer's fire.

AN ILLUSTRATION: Joel utilizes the metaphor of the locust plague and drought to launch an intensified call to repent in view of the coming invasion of Judah and the Day of the Lord, both present and future.

2:1. BLOW THE TRUMPET: In the ancient world, horns were used to gather people for special occasions or to warn of danger (see Exodus 19:13, 16, 19; 20:18; Numbers 10:1–10; Isaiah 27:13; Amos 3:6; Zephaniah 1:14–16; Zechariah 9:14; 1 Thessalonians 4:16). The term here refers to a ram's horn.

ZION: This term can refer either to earthly Jerusalem (see Isaiah 10:12) or the heavenly abode of God (see Hebrews 12:22). All seven occurrences in Joel, when taken in context (see 2:1, 15, 23, 32; 3:16–17, 21), refer to the earthly city.

THE DAY OF THE LORD: This is the second of five occurrences of this theme phrase in Joel (see 1:15; 2:11, 31; 3:14).

2. DARKNESS AND GLOOMINESS . . . CLOUDS AND THICK DARKNESS: These features describe the blackness of a locust invasion so thick that it blots out the sun with its deadly, living cloud of insects. Such terms are also common figures for misery and calamity in the Old Testament (see Isaiah 8:22; 60:2; Jeremiah 13:16; Amos 5:18, 20; Zephaniah 1:15) and past visitations of the Lord (see Exodus 10:12ff.; 19:16–19; 24:16; Deuteronomy 4:12; 5:22–23).

3–11. FIRE . . . HORSES . . . ARMY: In dramatic and vivid language, Joel compares the drought and locusts to fire, horses, and an invading army.

4–9. THEIR APPEARANCE IS LIKE . . . HORSES: The resemblance of the locust's head to that of a horse is striking—so much so that the prophet reiterates the word "appearance." Horses were not used for agricultural purposes in ancient times but were the most feared kind of military equipment (see Exodus 15:1ff., 19; Deuteronomy 20:1; Joshua 11:4). The simile continues with "like chariots" (verse 5), "like a strong people" (verse 5), "like mighty men" (verse 7), "like men of war" (verse 7), and "like a thief" (verse 9).

10. EARTH QUAKES . . . SUN AND MOON GROW DARK: The ground trembles as dust flies along with the growing devastation. Earthquakes and cosmic disruptions are well attested elsewhere as signs accompanying divine appearances (see Judges 5:4; Psalm 18:7; Jeremiah 4:23–26; Nahum 1:5–6; Matthew 24:7). So devastating are the locusts that they are associated with heavenly phenomena. Joel later refers to these signs (see 2:31; 3:15).

11. THE DAY OF THE LORD: This is the third of five occurrences (see 1:15; 2:1, 31; 3:14). There is a growing sense of severity with each successive mention.

12–14. TURN TO ME: Even in the midst of judgment, opportunity to repent was given. If the people would demonstrate genuine repentance, the Lord stood ready to forgive and bless. God had announced impending judgment, but the marred nation could be restored as a good vessel by God, who would hold off the judgment. By contrast, if the nation continued in sin, He would not bring the blessing desired (see Jeremiah 18:8–10). Tragically, pagan Ninevah repented and God relented (see Jonah 3:5–10), but Judah did not, and so the Lord would not.

15. BLOW . . . CONSECRATE . . . CALL: See Joel 1:14; 2:1.

16. THE ELDERS . . . THE CHILDREN: From oldest to youngest they were to come. The situation was so grave that even the groom and bride were exhorted to assemble (see Deuteronomy 24:5); consummation of the marriage could wait.

UNLEASHING THE TEXT

1) What impact did the locust swarm and the drought have on the land (see Joel 1:2–20)?

_____

_____

_____

_____

_____

2) Joel also describes a locust swarm in chapter 2, but in a different manner. What differences do you see between the descriptions in chapter 1:2–20 and 2:1–17?

_____

_____

_____

_____

_____

3) What do these chapters in Joel teach about the Day of the Lord?

_____

_____

_____

_____

_____

4) What was God's invitation to His people to escape the coming disaster (see Joel 2:12–17)?

_____

_____

_____

_____

EXPLORING THE MEANING

Teach the Next Generation About the Lord. Joel uses powerful imagery to describe the devastation that the locusts and drought had brought on the land. However, he begins his prophecy with an interesting set of commands: "Hear this, you elders, and give ear, all you inhabitants of the land! . . . Tell your children about it, let your children tell their children, and their children another generation" (1:2–3). God tells Joel that the elders—the civil and religious leaders—and inhabitants should have recognized that what they were facing had come about as a result of divine judgment. Now, they were to teach their children and grandchildren about the Lord's mighty acts. The same is true for us today. As Paul wrote, "Do not provoke your children to wrath, but bring them up in the training and admonition of the Lord" (Ephesians 6:4).

Do Not Rebel Against the Lord. The phrase "the day of the Lord" is used many times in Joel. But what does it actually mean? Joel's first mention of the phrase provides us with a clue: "Alas for the day! For the day of the LORD is at hand; it shall come as destruction from the Almighty" (1:15). Generally speaking, the Day of the Lord is a moment in which God pours out His wrath on mankind. In some circumstances, this "day" referrs to a localized time in which God punishes a specific person or people group. However, the same phrase can also point forward to the end of the age, when God pours out His wrath against evil during the Tribulation and the Second Coming of Christ. Importantly, the day of God's judgment is a fearsome event—but only for those who rebel against God and resist His grace. For God's children, the Day of the Lord is when evil is punished, justice accomplished, and the doors of God's blessing opened.

Return to the Lord with All Your Heart. As we have seen, the prophets often delivered a message of God's impending judgment and wrath. These messages were consistent with God's character, "for the LORD is a God of justice" (Isaiah 30:18), and He punishes evil in all its forms. Yet God is also merciful, and His primary desire is for rebels to lay down their arms and sinners to repent. Even amidst Joel's prophecies about the Day of the Lord, Joel included this aspect of God's character: "'Now, therefore,' says the LORD, 'Turn to Me with all your heart, with fasting, with weeping, and with mourning.' . . . For He is gracious and merciful, slow to anger, and of great kindness; and He relents from doing harm" (2:12–13). We all sin at times and "fall short of the glory of God" (Romans 3:23). The remedy for our sinful acts is to repent and return to a right relationship with God—to love Him and serve Him with our whole heart.

REFLECTING ON THE TEXT

5) What are some ways that God convicts you and make you aware of your sins?

_____

_____

_____

_____

_____

_____

6) Why does God make it a point to teach future generations about Him?

_____

_____

_____

_____

_____

_____

7) Why is it necessary for God to punish evildoers and those who are rebellious against Him? What would our future be like if there were no consequences for rejecting God?

_____

_____

_____

_____

8) Jesus said, "Love the LORD your God with all your heart, with all your soul, with all your mind, and with all your strength" (Mark 12:30). What does this mean? What does it look like?

_____

_____

_____

_____

PERSONAL RESPONSE

9) What can you share with others this week about how God has been faithful to you?

_____

_____

_____

_____

10) What is one way this week you will seek to "draw near to God" so that "He will draw near to you" (James 4:8)? What do you need to shift in your priorities to make this happen?

_____

_____

_____

_____

10

THE FUTURE DAY OF THE LORD

Joel 2:18–3:21

DRAWING NEAR

Write down some examples of good news that you have received in recent months. How do you typically respond when you hear such good news?

_____

_____

_____

_____

_____

_____

_____

_____

_____

_____

_____

_____

_____

_____

_____

_____

_____

_____

_____

THE CONTEXT

One of the elements of biblical prophecy that can make it difficult to follow is the presence of "layers" within the text. Many times, a prophetic statement or vision will touch on several different time periods: (1) the present time of the original hearer, (2) what would be the future for that original audience but is the past for us, and (3) the future for us as modern readers.

An example of this is found in Joel. The immediate context of Joel's prophecy was the devastating invasion of locusts that had decimated Judah's crops. "The field is wasted, the land mourns; for the grain is ruined" (1:10). However, Joel's vision also pointed forward to the future invasion of Judah by the armies of Babylon—"a people . . . great and strong" (2:2)—who would swarm over Jerusalem's walls in numbers similar to those of a swarm of locusts.

Yet even beyond this, Joel's prophecy points forward to God's *ultimate* judgment against sin and evil, which will occur at some point in the future in what is called the "Day of the Lord." As we come to the second half of Joel 2, specifically verse 18, we reach this moment when the prophetic text shifts decisively in terms of its intended timeline. From this point onward, the focus of Joel's prophecy moves from present judgment to future restoration.

KEYS TO THE TEXT

Read Joel 2:18–3:21, noting the key words and phrases indicated below.

> *MATERIAL AND SPIRITUAL RESTORATION: Joel makes a decisive transition in his prophecy, devoting the remainder of the book to future restoration.*

2:18. THEN THE LORD WILL BE ZEALOUS: This assumes an interval of time between verse 17 and verse 18 during which Israel repented. As a result of her repentance, the three major concerns of Joel 1:1–2:17 are answered by the Lord: (1) physical restoration (2:21–27), (2) spiritual restoration (2:28–32), and (3) national restoration (3:1–21).

19–27. REPROACH . . . SHAME: "No reproach" among the nations (verse 19) and "never be put to shame" (verses 26–27) are absolute statements that could only be fulfilled in the far future. See Joel 3:17.

20. BUT I WILL REMOVE . . . THE NORTHERN ARMY: Although some have viewed this as a reference to the locusts, it is more likely referring to a military

invasion by a country coming down from the north of Israel (see Ezekiel 38:6, 15; 39:2). That future army will be driven into the eastern sea (Dead Sea) and the western sea (Mediterranean Sea).

21–24. DO NO BE AFRAID, YOU BEASTS OF THE FIELD: Reminiscent of Joel 1:18–20, the former situation had been reversed. The animals were admonished to be afraid no longer.

23–24. FORMER . . . LATTER RAIN: The former rains came in October–December to prepare the seedbed and assist germination, while the latter rains came in March–May to provide ample moisture for the grain and fruit crops to be rich and full.

25. CRAWLING . . . CONSUMING . . . CHEWING LOCUST: See Joel 1:4.

27. I AM IN THE MIDST OF ISRAEL: This promised return would be a reversal of the Lord's departure (see Ezekiel 8–11).

28–32. IT SHALL COME TO PASS: Peter would later quote this passage in his sermon on the Day of Pentecost in Jerusalem (see Acts 2:16–21). Joel's prophecy will not be completely fulfilled until the millennial kingdom. But Peter, by using it, revealed that Pentecost was a pre-fulfillment, a taste of what would happen in the millennial kingdom when the Spirit is poured out on all flesh.

28. AFTERWARD: The abundance of material blessings would be followed by the outpouring of spiritual blessings. When coupled with the other temporal phrases within the passage ("in those days" [verse 29] and "before the coming of the great and awesome day of the LORD" [verse 31]), the term points to a Second Advent fulfillment time frame.

ALL FLESH: Since the context is "your sons and your daughters," the phrase "all flesh" best refers to the house of Israel only. The other nations are the recipients of God's wrath, not the effusion of His Spirit (see Joel 3:2, 9ff.).

30–31. BEFORE . . . DAY OF THE LORD: This is the fourth appearance of this phrase (see 1:15; 2:1, 11; 3:14). Unmistakable heavenly phenomena will signal the imminent arrival of God's wrath in the Day of the Lord (see verse 10; see also Matthew 24:29–31).

32. WHOEVER CALLS ON THE NAME OF THE LORD: Paul would later quote this verse in Romans 10:13 to emphasize that salvation is available for people of all nations and races.

REMNANT: In spite of the nation's sin, God promised to fulfill His unconditional covenants (Noahic covenant, Abrahamic covenant, priestly covenant, Davidic covenant, and New Covenant). A future remnant of Jews will inherit

God's promised blessings (see Isaiah 10:20–22; 11:11, 16; Jeremiah 31:7; Micah 2:12; Zephaniah 3:13; Romans 9:27).

NATIONAL RESTORATION: Joel now begins to relate the national restoration of Israel, in which the people will be regathered to the land.

3:2. GATHER ALL NATIONS: The nations of the world will be gathered to Jerusalem to the battle of Armageddon (see Zechariah 12:3; 14:2; Revelation 16:16; 19:11–21).

VALLEY OF JEHOSHAPHAT: The name means "Yahweh judges" (see verses 12, 14). Although the exact location of this valley is unknown, other prophets spoke of this judgment as occurring near Jerusalem (see Ezekiel 38–39; Daniel 11:45; Zechariah 9:14ff.; 12:1ff.). This judgment of the nations includes the event that Jesus would later describe in Matthew 25:31–46.

SCATTERED . . . DIVIDED: This has been the continual, historical circumstances of the Jews ever since the Babylonian deportation (605–586 BC) until this very time, making this divine promise yet future in accomplishment.

4. TYRE . . . SIDON: Important Phoenician seaports located on the Mediterranean Sea. Tyre was located about thirty-five miles north of Mount Carmel and twenty-eight miles west of Mount Hermon. Alexander the Great would ultimately conquer this stronghold in 330 BC (see Ezekiel 36:1–18). Sidon was located about twenty-two miles north of Tyre.

5–6. THE PEOPLE OF JUDAH . . . SOLD: The exact historical event referred to here is uncertain. Slave trading was a common practice among the Phoenicians and Philistines.

6. THE GREEKS: Although not prominent militarily, the Greeks were active in commerce on the Mediterranean Sea during the ninth century BC.

7–8. RETURN YOUR RETALIATION: The reversal of fortunes would be startling. The victims themselves would be called on to be the avengers and instruments of the Lord's wrath (see Isaiah 11:12–14; Zechariah 12:8).

8. SABEANS: Trading merchants who lived in Arabia (see 1 Kings 10; Jeremiah 6:20).

9–17. PROCLAIM THIS AMONG THE NATIONS: Joel resumes the theme of verses 1–3, the gathering of the nations to the earthly courtroom, the Valley of Jehoshaphat. The sentence has been handed down, and the Judge orders His agents to ready the scene for the execution.

10. PLOWSHARES . . . PRUNING HOOKS: Just the opposite will result after God judges the nations. See note on Micah 4:3.

12. VALLEY OF JEHOSHAPHAT: See note on verse 2.

13. THE HARVEST . . . THE WINEPRESS: This is a figurative scene describing God's judgment in the far eschatological sense at the advent of Christ's millennial rule. See Revelation 14:14–20.

14. IN THE VALLEY OF DECISION: This location is the same as the Valley of Jehoshaphat where the sentence of God's judgment will be carried out (see verses 2, 12).

DAY OF THE LORD: This is the final of five occurances (1:5; 2:1, 11, 31).

15–16. THE SUN AND MOON: See Joel 2:10, 30–31. These are the cosmic signs that precede the coming eschatological Day of the Lord at the end of the Great Tribulation (see Matthew 24:29–30).

16. ROAR: Joel here writes that the Lord "roars" against the nations; in another prophecy given in Amos 1:2, God's wrath is directed primarily toward Israel. Amos, a shepherd, courageously warned the flock of God's pasture that they were in imminent danger from a roaring lion who turned out to be the ultimate Shepherd of the flock.

17. ZION MY HOLY MOUNTAIN: This will be the earthly location of God's presence in the millennial temple at Jerusalem (see Ezekiel 40–48).

EVER PASS THROUGH HER AGAIN: See Joel 2:19, 26–27. God has promised a future time when His glory in Judah will not be eclipsed. This time of ultimate peace and prosperity will be experienced after Christ conquers the world and sets up His millennial kingdom on earth (see Ezekiel 37:24–28; Matthew 24–25; Revelation 19).

18. VALLEY OF ACACIAS: Known for its acacia trees, the valley was situated on the northern shores of the Dead Sea and served as the final stopover for Israel prior to her entrance into the Promised Land (see Numbers 25:1; Joshua 2:1; 3:1). This valley is also the place to which the millennial river will flow (see Ezekiel 47:1–12; Zechariah 14:8).

19. EGYPT . . . EDOM: The prophets Isaiah (19:1–25), Jeremiah (46:1–26), and Ezekiel (chapters 29–32) expand on Egypt's judgment. Isaiah (21:11–12), Jeremiah (49:7–22), Ezekiel (25:12–14), Amos (1:11–12), and Obadiah (entire book) provide more detail on Edom's punishment.

20. JUDAH . . . FOREVER: This is in reference to Christ's millennial kingdom on earth, which is yet to be fulfilled.

21. ACQUIT THEM: The Hebrew word translated here as "acquit" is better translated "avenge." Thus, verse 21 picks up the thought from verse 19—that God will judge those who had shed Judah's blood without warrant.

ZION: See note on Joel 2:1.

UNLEASHING THE TEXT

1) What promises did God make to His people in Joel 2:18–27? Why would those promises have been especially important to Joel's original audience?

_____

_____

_____

_____

_____

_____

_____

2) What can we learn about the actions of the Holy Spirit from Joel 2:28–32?

_____

_____

_____

_____

_____

3) How should we understand the timing of the prophecies in Joel 3? What ages of history is the prophet here describing?

_____

_____

_____

_____

_____

_____

4) How would you summarize the overall theme or message of Joel's words to the nation of Israel in chapter 3?

_____

_____

_____

_____

_____

_____

_____

_____

EXPLORING THE MEANING

God Brings Physical Restoration. Joel's prophecy paints a picture of a broken people in need of God's restoration. The Lord set about this restoration process by outlining three steps that needed to occur—the first of which was physical restoration. As we have seen, the locust invasion had been devastating to Judah's economy and to its people. Furthermore, Judah was going to be trampled by the armies of Babylon and the city of Jerusalem destroyed. Even so, God promised a future day when that land and city would be restored: "So I will restore to you the years that the swarming locust has eaten.... You shall eat in plenty and be satisfied, and praise the name of the LORD your God" (Joel 2:25–26). God promises the same to us. While we may not experience physical restoration in this life, we have the assurance that one day, in eternity, "There shall be no more death ... no more pain" (Revelation 21:4).

God Brings Spiritual Restoration. Physical restoration was no doubt helpful for the people of Judah, but it was only the first step. God also promised to restore His people spiritually: "And it shall come to pass afterward that I will pour out My Spirit on all flesh; your sons and your daughters shall prophesy, your old men shall dream dreams, your young men shall see visions. And also on My menservants and on My maidservants I will pour out My Spirit in those days" (Joel 2:28–29). God provided a pre-fulfillment of this on the Day of Pentecost, when the Holy Spirit was poured out on the disciples (see Acts 2:1–4, 17–21). Jesus' death and resurrection has provided all people with access to the spiritual restoration we call *salvation*. Although we are stained "like scarlet" by sin, we can be made "white as snow" (Isaiah 1:18) through the blood of Christ. There will also be a time when the Jewish people will return to God and accept Jesus as their Messiah. This has not yet occurred, but it *will* take place one day in the future.

God Brings National Restoration. God's final promise of restoration involved Israel's status as a nation. If it is correct that Joel ministered c. 835–796 BC, then neither the kingdom of Israel nor the kingdom of Judah had yet been conquered by foreign powers. Those tragedies were likely unimaginable to Joel's original audience. Yet God knew those conquests would occur, and He promised that Israel's status as a nation on the world stage would one day be restored. Much of what Joel prophesied in chapter 3 has yet to occur, including God's judgment against the nations that harrassed Israel. But Joel's prophecy assures us that God not only restores individuals but also whole nations: "If My people who are called by My name will humble themselves, and pray and seek My face, and turn from their wicked ways, then I will hear from heaven, and will forgive their sin and heal their land" (2 Chronicles 7:14).

REFLECTING ON THE TEXT

5) The people of Judah were in need of physical restoration. Where do you see evidence of this same kind of need in the world today? What about in the church?

_____

_____

_____

_____

_____

_____

6) God also promised to restore His people spiritually. How does God's offer of salvation through Jesus Christ connect with this promise of spiritual restoration?

_____

_____

_____

_____

_____

_____

7) When will the events foretold in Joel 2:28–32 ultimately be fulfilled? In light of the timing of these events, should they be considered normative for today?

_____
_____
_____
_____
_____
_____
_____
_____

8) God also promised to bring national retoration to His people. What will determine whether the establishment of the State of Israel in 1948 was the fulfillment of prophecy?

_____
_____
_____
_____
_____
_____
_____
_____

PERSONAL RESPONSE

9) While the promise of spiritual restoration as a nation was made exclusively to Israel, the promise of salvation is made to everyone who believes in Jesus Christ. Who do you know who needs to be spiritually restored? What can you do in the hope that will happen?

_____
_____
_____
_____
_____
_____
_____

10) How often do you think of God's future plan to restore not only Israel but also the world? How would meditating on such things benefit your walk with Christ in the present?

_____

_____

_____

_____

_____

_____

_____

11

GOD'S JUDGMENT ON EDOM
Obadiah 1:1–21

DRAWING NEAR
What are some of the major causes of strife within your family? How does that impact you?

_____

_____

_____

_____

_____

_____

_____

_____

_____

_____

_____

_____

_____

_____

_____

_____

_____

_____

_____

_____

_____

THE CONTEXT

The relationship between the nations of Israel and Edom was complicated from the very beginning. Both nations found their patriarchs in the twin sons of Isaac. Esau, the firstborn, was given the nickname "Edom" because of his reddish appearance at birth and his apparent affinity for red stew (see Genesis 25:30). The Edomites grew out of his descendants, while the Israelites of course were the descendants of Jacob. (Importantly, Edom married several Canaanite women, so his descendants were mixed with other nations.)

Centuries later, the Israelites encountered the Edomites after the Exodus from Egypt. Having spent forty years wandering in the wilderness, the Israelites were finally on their way back to the Promised Land. Their intended road led through the territory of the Edomites, so Moses sent messengers to Edom's king describing their intention to pass peacefully through the land. He even offered to pay for any water or food consumed by the Israelites. The King of Edom refused, however, even sending his armies out to patrol the border and make sure the Israelites did not enter their land (see Numbers 20:14–21).

From that moment forward, Edom became an enemy of Israel. Later, when the people of Israel and Judah were carried into captivity by foreign armies, the Edomites stood by and watched, potentially gloating (see Psalm 137:7). Obadiah's prophecy seals Edom's fate by announcing God's judgment against them, along with reinforcing the future restoration of Israel.

KEYS TO THE TEXT

Read Obadiah 1:1–21, noting the key words and phrases indicated below.

> EDOM'S CRIMES AND PUNISHMENT: *This is the first of only two minor prophets (Jonah being the other) who addressed their message to nations other than Israel and Judah.*

1:1. THE VISION: The prophetic word often came from God in the form of a vision (see Isaiah 1:1; Micah 1:1; Nahum 1:1; Habakkuk 1:1).

THUS SAYS THE LORD GOD: Although the background of the prophet Obadiah is obscure, the source of his message is not. It was supernaturally given by God and was not motivated by unholy vengeance (see Jeremiah 49:14).

EDOM: The Edomites, descendants of Esau (see Genesis 25:30; 36:1ff.), had settled in the region south of the Dead Sea. They were almost annihilated by

David (see 2 Samuel 8:14) but won back independence during the reign of Ahaz (c. 735–715 BC). Their revenge was constant hostility to Israel (see Genesis 27:27–41; Isaiah 34:5–7).

ARISE . . . RISE UP AGAINST HER: The prophet had heard of a God-ordained, international plot to overthrow Edom. The selfish motives of Edom's enemies were divinely controlled by the Lord's "messengers" to serve His sovereign purposes (see Psalm 104:4).

2. I WILL MAKE YOU: God sovereignly rules over all nations (see Daniel 2:21; 4:17; see also Jeremiah 49:15).

3–4. WHO WILL BRING ME DOWN . . . I WILL BRING YOU DOWN: Edom's pride was answered decisively by the Sovereign Ruler (see Matthew 23:12). The calamity against Edom, though brought about by her enemies, was truly God's judgment of her pride (see Proverbs 16:18; 1 Corinthians 10:12). In spite of her economic prosperity and geographical impregnability, the God of Jacob would topple Esau's offspring (see Jeremiah 49:16).

3. THE CLEFTS OF THE ROCK: Dwelling in difficult mountain terrain, Edom's imposing, impregnable capital city of Petra was virtually inaccessible, giving her a sense of security and self-sufficiency. Deep, terrifying gorges emanating from peaks reaching 5,700 feet surrounded her like a fortress, generating a proud, false sense of security.

5–6. ROBBERS BY NIGHT: Because of the rugged terrain and very narrow access through the gorges, predatory attack could only come at night. Edom's attackers, by divine judgment, would not stop where normal thieves would have stopped. Instead, they would leave nothing (see Jeremiah 49:9).

6. ESAU: The personification of the nation Edom (see Jeremiah 49:10).

7. ALL THE MEN: Those conspiring against Edom (verse 1) were her allies ("men in your confederacy"), her neighbors ("men at peace with you"), and even the outlying tribes who benefited from Edom's prosperity ("those who eat your bread").

8. WISE MEN: Edom was known for her wise men and sages (see Jeremiah 49:7). Her location on the King's Highway provided her with intellectual stimulation from India, Europe, and North Africa.

9. MIGHTY MEN: See Jeremiah 49:22b.

TEMAN: A name derived from a grandson of Esau (see Genesis 36:11), it refers to a region in the northern part of Edom that was the home of Job's friend, Eliphaz (see Job 4:1). See note on Habakkuk 3:3.

10. VIOLENCE AGAINST . . . JACOB: Edom's opposition is in view, which began as Israel approached the land (see Numbers 20:14–21) and continued to Habakkuk's day. Because Jacob and Esau were brothers, this evil of Edom was made even more reprehensible (see Genesis 25:23; Malachi 1:3; Romans 9:10–13). "Slaughter" (verse 9) and shame for Edom will be just retribution for Edom's violence and slaughter against his brother's people.

11–14. YOU STOOD . . . REJOICED . . . LAID HANDS ON . . . CUT OFF: The charge of verse 10 is here amplified: (1) they "stood," withholding assistance (verse 11); (2) they "rejoiced" over Judah's downfall (verse 12; see also Psalms 83:4–6; 137:7); (3) they plundered the city (verse 13); and (4) they prevented the escape of her fugitives (verse 14).

12–14. YOU SHOULD NOT . . . NOR SHOULD YOU: There are eight detailed accusations in this section, each indicated by "not" or "nor." Ezekiel would later write that the Edomites had brought God's judgment on themselves by acting like a cheering section for the Babylonians when they devasted Judah in 588–586 BC (see Ezekiel 25:12–14), crying out, "Raze it, raze it" (Psalm 137:7; see also Lamentations 4:21–22).

JUDGMENT ON THE NATIONS AND ISRAEL'S FINAL TRIUMPH: God's near judgment of Edom in history (verses 1–14) was a preview of His far judgment on all nations (verses 15–16) who refuse to bow to His sovereignty.

16. MY HOLY MOUNTAIN: Zion, referring to Jerusalem (see verse 17).

DRINK, AND SWALLOW: Compare to Zechariah 12:2, where the Lord will make His people as a "cup of drunkenness" from which His enemies will be made to drink. This refers to the cup of God's wrath. Judah drank temporarily of judgment; Edom will drink "continually," with irreversible, permanent results (see Jeremiah 49:12).

17. THERE SHALL BE DELIVERANCE: A reversal of Judah's plight at the hands of the Edomites in verses 10–14 will come about when Messiah intercedes, establishes His millennial kingdom, and "holiness" prevails.

18–20. KINDLE THEM AND DEVOUR THEM: Those of Judah who remain (see verse 14) will be divinely empowered to "devour" (verse 18) and completely wipe out the "house of Esau" (see Zechariah 12:6; Isaiah 11:14; 34:5–17). When Messiah sets up His kingdom, the boundaries of the Davidic and Solomonic kingdoms will once again expand to include that promised to Jacob in his dream at Bethel (see Genesis 28:14), which reaffirmed God's promise to Abraham (see Genesis 12). This would include the south (mountains of Esau), the west (Philistia), the north (Ephraim . . . Samaria), and the east (Gilead).

18. HOUSE OF JACOB . . . HOUSE OF JOSEPH: Representatives of Abraham's seed.

20. CANAANITES: Those peoples who occupied the land before the Exodus.

ZAREPHATH: Also known as Sarepta (see Luke 4:26), this town was located on the Phoenician coast between Tyre and Sidon.

SEPHARAD: Not mentioned elsewhere in the Bible, the location is uncertain. Most rabbis identify it with Spain; others have suggested Sparta or Sardis.

21. SAVIORS SHALL COME . . . TO JUDGE: Just as the Lord raised up judges to deliver His people (see Nehemiah 9:27), so will He establish similar leaders to help rule in the millennial kingdom (see 1 Corinthians 6:2; Revelation 20:4).

THE KINGDOM SHALL BE THE LORD'S: When the nations are judged in the Day of the Lord, He will then set up His millennial kingdom, a theocracy in which He rules His people directly on earth (see Zechariah 14:49; Revelation 11:15).

UNLEASHING THE TEXT

1) What do we learn about the Edomites from Obadiah 1:1–9?

_____

_____

_____

_____

_____

_____

_____

2) How should we understand the grievances described in verses 10–14? What are some of the things that Edom had done to earn God's wrath?

_____

_____

_____

_____

_____

_____

_____

3) Both Zephaniah and Joel spoke of the Day of the Lord in their prophecies. What does Obadiah say about the Day of the Lord in verses 15–16?

_____

_____

_____

_____

_____

4) What promises did God make to the people of Israel in verses 17–21?

_____

_____

_____

_____

EXPLORING THE MEANING

Don't Rely on Your Own Strength. The Edomites of Obadiah's day lived in elevated crags within the mountains south of the Dead Sea. This elevated territory was like a fortress that helped them defend themselves from any would-be attackers. Indeed, the Edomites believed that they were beyond their enemies' reach, saying in their hearts, "Who will bring me down to the ground?" (verse 3). However, the Edomites' self-confidence was misplaced, as God Himself had arranged for their destruction. In our modern world, it is easy for us to feel overly confident in our abilities and security. We can come to the conclusion that our resources and ingenuity are so great that they can overcome any problem. But such thinking is dangerous! When we put our faith in our own strength, we are always headed for a fall. As the apostle Paul warned, "Therefore let him who thinks he stands take heed lest he fall" (1 Corinthians 10:12).

Doing Nothing Is a Big Deal to God. There are "sins of commission" and "sins of "omission." Sins of commission occur when we actively break God's commands or move away from His values—we sin by doing something wrong. Sins of omission occur when we fail to do something we know we should do—by not doing something we know to be right. As James wrote, "Therefore, to him who knows to do good and does not do it, to him it is sin" (4:17). We see this principle in operation in Obadiah. The Edomites, by refusing to aid their ancestral kindred during times of need, had made themselves a stench not only to God's people but to God Himself. Although they did not directly attack or harm the Israelites during those critical encounters, they did fail to help their "brothers." We have to remember this same principle in our lives. Most of us want to avoid doing what we know is wrong, but it has become acceptable in our culture to *not* do something right. Such an attitude does not align with God's desire for our lives.

Our Trials Are Only Temporary. The nations of Israel and Judah largely declined during the ministry of the prophets; their borders shrank, their prosperity waned (especially in comparison with all that Solomon had achieved), and both nations ultimately experienced military defeat and exile. These were major setbacks for God's people. Yet the end of Obadiah's prophecy reminds us that these setbacks will seem relatively minor when history reaches its endpoint: "But on Mount Zion there shall be deliverance, and there shall be holiness; the house of Jacob shall possess their possessions" (verse 17). The final five verses of Obadiah's prophecy describe the millennial kingdom, in which Christ will rule from Jerusalem as King over all the earth. As Paul would later state, our focus should not be on the troubles of this world but on the eternity that we will one day spend with Christ: "For our light affliction, which is but for a moment, is working for us a far more exceeding and eternal weight of glory" (2 Corinthians 4:17).

REFLECTING ON THE TEXT

5)   What is our culture's view of self-reliance? What are some of things in which people often place their trust and look to for security?

_____

_____

_____

_____

_____

6)   On a practical level, what does it look like for you to place your confidence in God rather than in yourself? What kind of life does that produce?

_____

_____

_____

_____

_____

7) In a sense, there is always something that we could be doing to advance God's kingdom on this earth. So how can you identify a moment when *not* doing something becomes sin?

_____

_____

_____

_____

_____

_____

8) What does it look like—on a practical level—to view the trials of this life as "light affliction" and instead focus on the "eternal weight of glory"?

_____

_____

_____

_____

_____

PERSONAL RESPONSE

9) In what areas of life are you in danger of self-reliance and overconfidence?

_____

_____

_____

_____

_____

_____

10) What will you do this week to contemplate the reality of your heavenly home?

_____

_____

_____

_____

_____

_____

_____

12

REVIEWING KEY PRINCIPLES

DRAWING NEAR
What have you appreciated or enjoyed most about this study? Why?

_____
_____
_____
_____
_____
_____
_____
_____
_____
_____
_____
_____
_____
_____
_____
_____
_____
_____
_____
_____
_____
_____
_____
_____

THE CONTEXT

Studying the prophets (both major and minor) often leads to the question, "Do we have prophets like those in the Old Testament operating within our world today?" The short answer is *no*. The reason for this, as the author of Hebrews explained, is that "God, who at various times and in various ways spoke in time past to the fathers by the prophets, has in these last days spoken to us by His Son, whom He has appointed heir of all things, through whom also He made the worlds" (Hebrews 1:1–2). Jesus, as our Messiah and Savior, fulfilled (in the sense of completed) the role of prophet; God spoke directly to us in the form of a man.

Similarly, believers in Christ are now indwelt with the Holy Spirit. Jesus said of the Holy Spirit, "He will teach you all things, and bring to your remembrance all things that I said to you" (John 14:26). He added, "When He, the Spirit of truth, has come, He will guide you into all truth; for He will not speak on His own authority, but whatever He hears He will speak; and He will tell you things to come" (John 16:13). God lives in us, speaks to us, and guides us personally. As Paul wrote, "God has sent forth the Spirit of His Son into your hearts" (Galatians 4:6).

Even so, there is great value in studying the writings of the Old Testament prophets. Sometimes, we may find it challenging to work through this particular section of the Bible, but we have to remember that servants such as Micah, Nahum, Zephaniah, Habakkuk, Joel, and Obadiah were not prophesying just for the benefit of their original audience. Rather, these "holy men of God spoke as they were moved by the Holy Spirit" (2 Peter 1:21). Their words were inspired by the Holy Spirit, which means they are profitable for all who follow God.

EXPLORING THE MEANING

God's Truth Always Prevails. The false prophets of Micah's day were advising him to "not prattle" (2:6). They wanted him to stop telling the people of God's truth so as not to upset the system of false idols, corrupt government, and unjust monetary practices that had been established in the land. This was a case of bad press potentially ruining their livelihood. What these false prophets failed to recognize is that God would not sit idly by as they went about their endeavors. As Micah said to them, "Because it is defiled, it shall destroy, yes, with utter destruction" (verse 10). God will always speak His truth into our lives to redirect us back to His ways. If we refuse to listen to His truth, we will suffer the consequences. The question for us is thus whether we will listen to God when He gently tells us that the way we are heading will lead to destruction. Will we turn our backs on that way of life or continue on and risk His judgment?

Beware the Pitfalls of Power. Micah did not shy away from calling out the rulers, priests, and prophets of Israel—all of whom carried the responsibility of leading the people toward the Lord God (see 3:9–12). Authority and power are always coupled with responsibility. Those who have wealth should use that wealth to further God's kingdom. Those who are influential should use that influence to bring people closer to God. Those who believe in Jesus and have a relationship with Him should demonstrate the love of Christ to others through the example of their lives. We are each to use the gifts that we have received from God in service to Jesus, our rightful King, and not for our own self-interests. As Peter wrote, "As each one has received a gift, minister it to one another, as good stewards of the manifold grace of God" (1 Peter 4:10).

The Time to Repent Is Now. The apostle Peter wrote, "The Lord is not slack concerning His promise, as some count slackness, but is longsuffering toward us, not willing that any should perish but that all should come to repentance" (2 Peter 3:9). God had been patient with Judah. He had sent His prophets to warn the people of what would happen if they did not turn from their sins. But the people had persisted in their idolatry, and now God's judgment was about to fall on them. Zephaniah's message to the people was thus, "The time to repent is now!" The same is true in our lives. God convicts us of our sins and gives us the opportunity to repent. But we need to recognize that He is being merciful and not delay in confessing our transgressions.

The Word of God Is Truth. One of the most powerful elements of Nahum's prophecy is the accuracy with which it foretold the eventual destruction of Nineveh. Remember that Nahum delivered this prophecy decades before the city was destroyed. Even so, he was able to comment on the different stages and horrors of the sack of Nineveh as if he had personally witnessed the events. For instance, Nahum said Nineveh would end "with an overflowing flood" (1:8), and this happened when the Tigris River overflowed, destroying enough of the city walls to allow the Babylonian army to invade. Nahum also prophesied the city would "be hidden" (3:11), and this proved true because the city was not rediscovered after its destruction until AD 1842. Nahum's accuracy was bad news for Nineveh but good news for followers of Christ, for it reveals that *all* God's words are true. We can trust the accuracy and truth of the Bible.

God Loves a Humble Heart. As we have seen, Habakkuk was deeply dismayed by the news that Babylon would serve as the instrument of justice against God's people in Judah. He asked the Lord, "Shall they therefore . . . continue to slay nations without pity?" (1:17). God answered that the Babylonians would also receive judgment for their wickedness—including their pride. The Lord added, "Behold the proud, his soul is not upright in him; but the just shall live by his faith" (2:4). This verse sets up an important dichotomy for us. We can live according to our own strength and resources, which leads to pride. Or we can submit to God's strength and resources, which requires faith. The Bible reveals where the first path leads: "Pride goes before destruction, and a haughty spirit before a fall" (Proverbs 16:18). But those who submit to the Lord in faith receive the promise that God "gives grace to the humble" (James 4:6).

Worship God for Who He Is. As limited human beings who worship a limitless God, we can fall into the error of defining our relationship with God by what He can do for us—worshiping Him not because of who He is but because of the blessings He provides. This leads to a transactional relationship, as if God were a divine vending machine. Early in Habakkuk, we find the prophet meditating on what he wants God to do; namely, punish the wicked in Judah. He then wants God to spare those same evildoers from the wrath of Babylon. But in Habakkuk 3, we find the prophet focusing more on God's attributes than His actions. Habakkuk praises God's nature and character, including both His mercy and strength. The psalm ends with a reflection on worshiping God even when circumstances are difficult: "Though the fig tree may not blossom, nor fruit be on the vines; though the labor of the olive may fail, and the fields yield no food; though the flock may be cut off from the fold, and there be no herd in the stalls—yet I will rejoice in the LORD, I will joy in the God of my salvation" (verses 17–18).

Return to the Lord with All Your Heart. As we have seen, the prophets often delivered a message of God's impending judgment and wrath. These messages were consistent with God's character, "for the LORD is a God of justice" (Isaiah 30:18), and He punishes evil in all its forms. Yet God is also merciful, and His primary desire is for rebels to lay down their arms and sinners to repent. Even amidst Joel's prophecies about the Day of the Lord, Joel included this aspect of God's character: "'Now, therefore,' says the LORD, 'Turn to Me with all your heart, with fasting, with weeping, and with mourning.' . . . For He is gracious and merciful, slow to anger, and of great kindness; and He relents from doing harm" (2:12–13). We all sin at times and "fall short of the glory of God" (Romans 3:23). The remedy for our sinful acts is to repent and return to a right relationship with God—to love Him and serve Him with our whole heart.

Doing Nothing Is a Big Deal to God. There are "sins of commission" and "sins of "omission." Sins of commission occur when we actively break God's commands or move away from His values—we sin by doing something wrong. Sins of omission occur when we fail to do something we know we should do—by not doing something we know to be right. As James wrote, "Therefore, to him who knows to do good and does not do it, to him it is sin" (4:17). We see this principle in operation in Obadiah. The Edomites, by refusing to aid their ancestral kindred during times of need, had made themselves a stench not only to God's people but to God Himself. Although they did not directly attack or harm the Israelites during those critical encounters, they did fail to help their "brothers." We have to remember this same principle in our lives. Most of us want to avoid doing what we know is wrong, but it has become acceptable in our culture to *not* do something right. Such an attitude does not align with God's desire for our lives.

UNLEASHING THE TEXT

1) Which of the prophetic books covered in this study did you enjoy most? Why?

_____

_____

_____

_____

_____

_____

_____

_____

_____

_____

2) What did you find especially challenging in your study of Micah, Nahum, Zephaniah, Habakkuk, Joel, and Obadiah? What was especially rewarding?

_____

_____

_____

_____

3) How did your study of these minor prophets add to your understanding of God's nature and character?

_____

_____

_____

_____

_____

4) Why do justice and judgment remain important themes even in our modern Church Age that is marked by God's grace?

_____

_____

_____

_____

PERSONAL RESPONSE

5) Have you repented of your sin and placed your faith in the finished work of Jesus Christ? Do you strive to put off sin and put on righteousness out of your love for Him? Explain.

_____

_____

_____

_____

_____

_____

6) What sins have you been most convicted of during this study? What will you do to address those sins? What will that look like over time? Be specific.

_____

_____

_____

_____

_____

_____

_____

7) What steps can you take to share what you have learned throughout this study with others who need to hear it?

_____

_____

_____

_____

_____

_____

8) In what areas do you hope to grow spiritually over the coming weeks and months? What steps will you need to take in order to achieve that growth?

_____

_____

_____

_____

_____

_____

_____

If you would like to continue in your study of the Old Testament, read the next title in this series: _Zechariah, Haggai, and Malachi: A Call to Rebuild._

Also Available in the
John MacArthur Bible Study Series

The MacArthur Bible Studies provide intriguing examinations of the whole of Scripture. Each of the 35 guides (16 Old Testament and 19 New Testament) incorporates extensive commentary, detailed observations on overriding themes, and probing questions to help you study the Word of God.

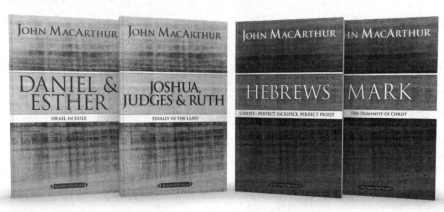

Available now at your favorite bookstore.
More volumes coming soon.

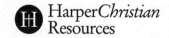

Harper*Christian* Resources